William Faulkner's *The Sound and the Fury* met with only limited success when published in 1929, probably due to its fragmented, non-chronological structure. Since, however, it has become one of the most popular of Faulkner's novels serving as a litmus paper upon which critical approaches have tested themselves. In the introduction to this volume Noel Polk traces the critical responses to the novel from the time of its publication to the present day. The essays that follow present contemporary reassessments of *The Sound and the Fury* from a variety of critical perspectives. Dawn Trouard offers us the women of *The Sound and the Fury*, reading against the grain of the predominant critical tradition which sees the women through the lens of masculine cultural biases. Donald M. Kartiganer comes to terms with the ways in which the novel simultaneously attracts readers and resists readings. Richard Godden discusses the relationship between incest and miscegenation. Noel Polk examines closely the way Faulkner experiments with language.

NEW ESSAYS ON THE SOUND AND THE FURY

★ The American Novel ★

GENERAL EDITOR

Emory Elliott
University of California, Riverside

Other books in the series:

New Essays on The Scarlet Letter
New Essays on The Great Gatsby
New Essays on Adventures of Huckleberry Finn
New Essays on Moby-Dick
New Essays on Uncle Tom's Cabin
New Essays on The Red Badge of Courage
New Essays on The Sun Also Rises
New Essays on A Farewell to Arms
New Essays on The American
New Essays on The Portrait of a Lady
New Essays on Light in August
New Essays on The Awakening
New Essays on Invisible Man
New Essays on Native Son
New Essays on Their Eyes Were Watching God
New Essays on The Grapes of Wrath
New Essays on Winesburg, Ohio
New Essays on Sister Carrie
New Essays on The Rise of Silas Lapham
New Essays on The Catcher in the Rye
New Essays on White Noise
New Essays on The Crying of Lot 49
New Essays on Walden
New Essays on Poe's Major Tales
New Essays on Hawthorne's Major Tales
New Essays on Daisy Miller and The Turn of the Screw
New Essays on Rabbit, Run

New Essays on The Sound and the Fury

Edited by
Noel Polk

CAMBRIDGE UNIVERSITY PRESS
Cambridge, New York, Melbourne, Madrid, Cape Town, Singapore, São Paulo

Cambridge University Press
The Edinburgh Building, Cambridge CB2 2RU, UK

Published in the United States of America by Cambridge University Press, New York

www.cambridge.org
Information on this title: www.cambridge.org/9780521451147

First published 1993

A catalogue record for this publication is available from the British Library

Library of Congress Cataloguing in Publication data

New essays on The Sound and the fury / edited by Noel Polk.
p. cm. – (The American novel)
ISBN 0-521-45114-0. – ISBN 0-521-45734-3 (pbk.)
1. Faulkner, William, 1897–1962. Sound and the fury.
1. Polk, Noel. II. Series.
PS3511.A86S8 1993
813′.52 – dc20 93-568

ISBN-13 978-0-521-45114-7 hardback
ISBN-10 0-521-45114-0 hardback

ISBN-13 978-0-521-45734-7 paperback
ISBN-10 0-521-45734-3 paperback

Transferred to digital printing 2005

Contents

Series Editor's Preface

In literary criticism the last twenty-five years have been particularly fruitful. Since the rise of the New Criticism in the 1950s, which focused attention of critics and readers upon the text itself – apart from history, biography, and society – there has emerged a wide variety of critical methods which have brought to literary works a rich diversity of perspectives: social, historical, political, psychological, economic, ideological, and philosophical. While attention to the text itself, as taught by the New Critics, remains at the core of contemporary interpretation, the widely shared assumption that works of art generate many different kinds of interpretations has opened up possibilities for new readings and new meanings.

Before this critical revolution, many works of American literature had come to be taken for granted by earlier generations of readers as having an established set of recognized interpretations. There was a sense among many students that the canon was established and that the larger thematic and interpretative issues had been decided. The task of the new reader was to examine the ways in which elements such as structure, style, and imagery contributed to each novel's acknowledged purpose. But recent criticism has brought these old assumptions into question and has thereby generated a wide variety of original, and often quite surprising, interpretations of the classics, as well as of rediscovered works such as Kate Chopin's *The Awakening*, which has only recently entered the canon of works that scholars and critics study and that teachers assign their students.

The aim of The American Novel Series is to provide students of American literature and culture with introductory critical guides to American novels and other important texts now widely read and studied. Usually devoted to a single work, each volume begins with an introduction by the volume editor, a distinguished authority on the text. The introduction presents details of the work's composition, publication history, and contemporary reception, as well as a survey of the major critical trends and readings from first publication to the present. This overview is followed by four or five original essays, specifically commissioned from senior scholars of established reputation and from outstanding younger critics. Each essay presents a distinct point of view, and together they constitute a forum of interpretative methods and of the best contemporary ideas on each text.

It is our hope that these volumes will convey the vitality of current critical work in American literature, generate new insights and excitement for students of American literature, and inspire new respect for and new perspectives upon these major literary texts.

Emory Elliott
University of California, Riverside

1

Introduction

NOEL POLK

THE SOUND AND THE FURY is the quintessential American high modernist text. For over sixty years now, but especially since its sudden "discovery" by readers and critics in the late forties and early fifties, it has attracted the attention of most major critics and nearly every major critical movement. It has been a sort of litmus paper on which critical approaches have tested themselves, from Marxism to New Criticism, to Structuralism and Poststructuralism, Deconstruction, Psychoanalytics, Linguistics, Feminism, and New Historicism, all of which seem to find it among the sine qua nons of its particular approach. Because it is so rich, so astonishingly full of the mainstreams of twentieth-century culture, it stands in a reciprocal relationship to us: it opens itself up to economic, historical, philosophical, religious, cultural, and social analyses, and in its reflecting turn enables us to see how profoundly all these streams are related to each other, and to us. Each of these approaches has enriched our understanding of the novel (though not all readings have done so), and it has generously given us back ourselves. Even so, if the amount of current critical activity involving *The Sound and the Fury* is any indication, it remains a Matterhorn of seemingly inexhaustible splendor, with unscaled faces we haven't even discovered yet.

Faulkner's fourth completed novel, *The Sound and the Fury* comes in his career at the end of more than a decade of feverish reading and writing. In the late teens and early twenties he wrote reams of derivative poetry that reflected his absorption of the language and concerns of the European Romantics, of the fin de siècle poets, of the essential thinkers during the period of his intellectual gestation: Freud, Einstein, Bergson, Frazer; the literary modernists:

Pound, Anderson, Dos Passos, and especially Joyce and Eliot. Thanks partly to the mentorship of Oxford, Mississippi, lawyer Phil Stone, partly to his friendship with writers like Stark Young and Sherwood Anderson, partly to his travels, and partly to the University of Mississippi Library, Faulkner had access to a wide range of the literature of the past and to the most avant garde of current writing, all of which he devoured.

His own accounts of the origins of *The Sound and the Fury* are eyeball-deep in metaphors economic, romantic, modernist, and paternal:

> When I began it I had no plan at all. I wasn't even writing a book. I was thinking of books, publication, only in the reverse, in saying to myself, I wont have to worry about publishers liking or not liking this at all. Four years before I had written Soldiers' Pay. It didn't take long to write and it got published quickly and made me about five hundred dollars. I said, Writing novels is easy. You dont make much doing it, but it is easy. I wrote Mosquitoes. It wasn't quite so easy to write and it didn't get published quite as quickly and it made me about four hundred dollars. I said, Apparently there is more to writing novels, being a novelist, than I thought. I wrote Sartoris. It took much longer, and the publisher refused it at once. But I continued to shop it about for three years with a stubborn and fading hope, perhaps to justify the time which I had spent writing it. This hope died slowly, thought it didn't hurt at all. One day I seemed to shut a door between me and all publishers' addresses and book lists. I said to myself, Now I can write. Now I can make myself a vase like that which the old Roman kept at his bedside and wore the rim slowly away with kissing it. So I, who had never had a sister and was fated to lose my daughter in infancy, set out to make myself a beautiful and tragic little girl.[1]

He wrote this in 1933, as part of an introduction to a proposed new edition of the novel which never got beyond the planning stages. The introduction, extant in several versions, was not published until 1972, but throughout his career, especially in the 1950s when as a Nobel Laureate he was lionized and interviewed everywhere he went, he continued to mine the vein he had opened there, and spun variations on this basic story, creating a sort of myth about the novel's writing and conception. His oft-cited interview with Jean Stein in the *Paris Review* in the mid-1950s is his most elaborate and well-known version of the novel's composition:

> It began with a mental picture. I didn't realize at the time it was symbolical. The picture was of the muddy seat of a little girl's drawers in a pear tree where she could see through a window where her grandmother's funeral was taking place and report what was happening to her brothers on the ground below. By the time I explained who they were and what they were doing and how her pants got muddy, I realized it would be impossible to get all of it into a short story and that it would have to be a book. And then I realized the symbolism of the soiled pants, and that image was replaced by the one of the fatherless and motherless girl climbing down the rainpipe to escape from the only home she had, where she had never been offered love or affection or understanding. I had already begun to tell it through the eyes of the idiot child since I felt that it would be more effective as told by someone capable only of knowing what happened, but not why. I saw that I had not told the story that time. I tried to tell it again, the same story through the eyes of another brother. That was still not it. I told it for the third time through the eyes of the third brother. That was still not it. I tried to gather the pieces together and fill in the gaps by making myself the spokesman. It was still not complete, not until 15 years after the book was published when I wrote as an appendix to another book the final effort to get the story told and off my mind, so that I myself could have some peace from it. It's the book I feel tenderest towards. I couldn't leave it alone, and I never could tell it right, though I tried hard and would like to try again, though I'd probably fail again.[2]

In other accounts, Faulkner claimed that it began in a short story about the Compson children, a story

> without plot, of some children being sent away from the house during the grandmother's funeral. They were too young to be told what was going on and they saw things only incidentally to the childish games they were playing.[3]

Most commentators have taken Faulkner a bit more literally in these comments than is wise – or necessary. If *The Sound and the Fury* is the quintessential American high modernist novel, it is probably sensible to take Faulkner's claim to have "shut the door between [himself] and all publishers' addresses" as the quintessential modernist metaphor, in its implicit assertion of High Art's right and need to exist for itself alone, its rejection of any relationship between art and economic motive, its claim not to have to submit itself to any market, much less one geared to the debased tastes of a bourgeois public. All his comments about the conception and writing of the novel come at least four or five years after its publication, and so probably ought be taken less as fact than as his retrospective rumination about a profoundly important experience, a warm and loving distillation of that experience into metaphors that would allow him somehow to retain and evoke at will the passion that writing *The Sound and the Fury* gave him. That passion was something he truly seemed to cherish for the remainder of his life. Nor, he claimed, doubtless also metaphorically, did the ecstasy he felt in writing the Benjy section ever return in any of his other books. He never again felt "that eager and joyous faith and anticipation of surprise which the yet unmarred sheets beneath my hand held inviolate and unfailing."[4] Of course it may well be that he conceived and wrote the novel exactly as he later described; in any case, legions of critics have found his description of the muddy seat of Caddy's drawers a very evocative, and provocative, entrance into the novel's various structures and meanings, and much fruitful discussion has recently emerged from considerations of Caddy as the novel's absent center, its absent presence. But whether he was speaking metaphorically or not, clearly writing *The Sound and the Fury* was an immensely powerful experience for him, an experience by which he seemed to have defined himself as a writer, and he must have taken enormous satisfaction in its accomplishment, no matter what he later said about its being his "most splendid failure."[5] It should not surprise us to see how easily the master mythmaker mythologized the creation of his favorite book.

Whether the image of Caddy's drawers was in fact the cohering center of the novel's conception, we do not know. What we *do* know about the novel's antecedents might suggest something a bit more prosaic. Though he completed the typing of *The Sound and the Fury* in October of 1928, there is some evidence that fictional materials which he would eventually weave into it had been on his mind for several years at least. It is certainly not necessary to believe that he actually had in mind the *Sound and Fury* that we know as he worked through these materials, or even that he saw them as related to one another. But as Faulkner's letters home from New Haven in the spring and early summer of 1918 demonstrate, even then he was, willy-nilly, storing up materials which he would eventually incorporate into *The Sound and the Fury.*[6] As nearly every historian of this text has pointed out, a crude preliminary version of Benjy Compson appears in one of the sketches, "The Kingdom of God," that Faulkner published in the New Orleans *Times-Picayune* in early 1925. Carvel Collins claims to have been told by one of his sources that Faulkner read or told him a story about the Compson children in Paris in 1925.[7] This is possible, though by no means provable. Some fictions we do know he worked on in Paris – *Elmer* (1925; published 1983) certainly, and probably *Sanctuary* (1931) – and a pseudomedieval allegory entitled *Mayday* (1926; published 1977) has significant and specific affinities of theme, character, and mise-en-scène with *The Sound and the Fury,* as does *Flags in the Dust,* completed in 1927 and published two years later in a truncated version as *Sartoris* (1929). Moreover, similar affinities of theme and character might argue that *Flags, Sanctuary,* and *The Sound and the Fury* emerge from a single matrix in Faulkner's imagination. Certainly *Flags* and *Sanctuary,* especially in its original version,[8] are closely related, so closely that bits of the materials deleted from *Flags* to make *Sartoris* turn up in the original version of *Sanctuary,* salvaged as it were from what he doubtless assumed would be lost. *Sanctuary* was mainly written in the spring of 1929, while Cape and Smith were copyediting *The Sound and the Fury.* At some point during that spring Faulkner put *Sanctuary* aside long enough to revise extensively and retype forty-one pages of the Quentin section of *The Sound and the Fury,* so that in important ways *Sanctuary* and *The Sound and the Fury* are practically simultaneous, and I have suggested elsewhere that Horace Benbow, the Prufrockian hero of *Sanctuary* and *Flags,* is a forty-three-year-old Quentin Compson, what Quentin would have become had he lived that long.[9] Furthermore, if we can reasonably suspect that the letter Faulkner wrote to his mother from Paris in 1925 describing something he had just written about the Luxembourg Gardens and rain and death[10] is a version of *Sanctuary*'s final vision of Temple Drake in the Luxembourg Gardens, it may be worth speculating that the origins of that matrix lie in the materials of *Sanctuary.* Clearly he conceived of *Sanctuary* as a highly experimental novel. The holograph manuscript of that novel – with its thousands of revisions, its continual shift of passage after passage, page after page – and the revised galleys – characterized by the same restless shifting of large blocks of material – demonstrate how very difficult *Sanctuary* was to get on paper in a form that satisfied him. The extant materials thus make it possible to speculate that Faulkner worked on it sporadically through the late twenties, couldn't get the Horace Benbow–Temple Drake material to coalesce, then defaulted into *Flags,* a much more traditional novel. After *Flags,* something magical, perhaps even the discovery of Caddy's muddy drawers in a tree, moved him into *The Sound and the Fury.* The experience of writing *The Sound and the Fury* then released him to complete work on the Benbow–Temple Drake book, which in its "original version" was a book exclusively about Horace Benbow. In its revised, post–*Sound and Fury* avatar, Horace shares the spotlight with Temple.

Central to these early fictions is not a little girl with muddy drawers, but rather an effete, idealistic young man trying to find his way through a modernist tangle of postwar despair, historical disfranchisement and disillusionment, and Freudian-psychosexual problemata; all except the idiot in "The Kingdom of God" are recognizable avatars of Quentin Compson. Even so, it's not difficult to imagine that the discovery of Caddy's muddy drawers in that tree provided Faulkner a riveting imaginative center for all that masculine suffering to cohere around, a powerful narrative locus which gave him what he needed to organize the materials of his imagination.

The main thrust of the writing of *The Sound and the Fury* came in 1928. Faulkner finished typing it in October of that year in New York, apparently while Wasson edited *Flags in the Dust.* As Wasson – and legend – would have it, Faulkner erupted into Wasson's room one morning, tossed the manuscript on his bed, and said "Read this one, Bud. . . . It's a real son of a bitch."[11] Faulkner sent the ribbon typescript directly to his friend Harrison Smith, an editor at Harcourt, Brace, which was to publish *Sartoris*, the edited version of *Flags*. Harcourt rejected the new novel on February 15, 1929.[12] In the meantime, Smith left Harcourt to go into partnership with the British publisher Jonathan Cape, who wanted an American subsidiary. Smith took Faulkner's new typescript with him and the new firm of Jonathan Cape and Harrison Smith executed a contract for *The Sound and the Fury* on February 18, 1929, barely three days after Harcourt's rejection. Cape & Smith lost no time getting the novel into production, but the editing and the proofreading did not go smoothly. After entrusting the completed ribbon typescript to Smith, Faulkner apparently began tinkering with the carbon typescript text of Quentin's monologue, which he had retained (with few exceptions, the pages of the Quentin section are the only ones in the carbon typescript with holograph revision). Faulkner revised some passages of this section extensively, polished and pruned others, and experimented with several possibilities for punctuation, italicization, and phrasing.[13] When he received the copyedited ribbon typescript, he retyped forty-one pages completely and substituted the new ribbon copies in the setting copy he returned to Smith. In the carbon copy he was keeping he carefully replaced the worked-over and revised carbon pages with the newly typed carbons; the old carbons are not known to exist.

Faulkner probably received galleys just as he was getting married and leaving for his honeymoon. The only available correspondence concerning the proofreading is undated, but the return address is Pascagoula, Mississippi.[14] It is not clear from this correspondence whether he received at this or any other time any proof other than that for the Benjy section; his only comments are about the text of that part of the novel. Wasson, assigned to edit the new novel, changed a number of the details of the text. Faulkner took issue with him, however, over only one major problem in the proof of the Benjy section: Wasson changed all of Faulkner's italics to roman type, and proposed to indicate time shifts by line spaces in the text. Wasson's presumptuous editing of the first section prompted Faulkner's now well-known letter in which he patiently, but in no uncertain terms, told Wasson to put it back the way it was, or nearly so: "I know you mean well, but so do I."

This letter, with its detailed explanation of the alternating italic and roman passages, is a source of joy for a critic:

> I received the proof. It seemed pretty tough to me, so I corrected it as written, adding a few more italics where the original seemed obscure on second reading. Your reason for the change, i.e., that with italics only 2 different dates were indicated I do not think sound for 2 reasons. First, I do not see that the use of breaks clarifies it any more; second, there are more than 4 dates involved. The ones I recall off-hand are: Damuddy dies. Benjy is 3. (2) His name is changed. He is 5. (3) Caddy's wedding. He is 14. (4) He tries to rape a young girl and is castrated. 15. (5) Quentin's death. (6) His father's death. (7) A visit to the cemetery at 18. (7) [sic] The day of the anecdote, he is 33. These are just a few I recall. So your reason explodes itself.
>
> But the main reason is, a break indicates an objective change in tempo, while the objective picture here should be a continuous whole, since the thought transference is subjective; i.e., in Ben's mind and not in the reader's eye. I think italics are necessary to establish for the reader Benjy's confusion; that unbroken-surfaced confusion of an idiot which is outwardly a dynamic and logical coherence. To gain this, by using breaks it will be necessary to write an induction for each transference. I wish publishing was advanced enough to use colored ink for such, as I argued with you and Hal in the speak-easy that day. But the form in which you now have it is pretty tough. It presents a most dull and poorly articulated picture to my eye. If something must be done, it were better to re-write this whole section objectively, like the 4th section. I think it is rotten, as is. But if you wont have it so, I'll just have to save the idea until publishing grows up to it. Anyway, change all the italics. You overlooked one of them. Also, the parts written in italics will all have to be punctuated again. You'd better see to that, since you're all for coherence. And dont make any more additions to the script, bud. I know you mean well, but so do I. I effaced the 2 or 3 you made. . . .
>
> I hope you will think better of this. Your reason above disproves itself. I purposely used italics for both actual scenes and remembered scenes for the reason, not to indicate the different dates of happenings, but merely to permit the reader to anticipate a thought-transference, letting the recollection postulate its own date. Surely you see this.[15]

Faulkner's adamant concerns with such details suggests how intimately related to the novel's themes he considered the text's visual qualities to be, how relevant to its meanings; his savagely ironic comment that he might have to rewrite the Benjy section more conventionally if publishing were not "grown up" enough to handle it as it was, likewise suggests that at least prior to publication he was not quite so indifferent to publishers or the reading public as his postpublication comments about shutting the doors between himself and his publishers would indicate.

The Sound and the Fury was published on October 7, 1929, in a text marred by surprisingly few errors, astonishingly few, given its textual difficulties and the amount of repair done to the Benjy section in galleys. It was read and appreciated by a select few writers and readers who seemed to have some sense of what Faulkner had done. The Grabhorn Press proposed a new edition in the early thirties, one which would publish the Benjy section in three different colors to indicate time shifts, and for which Faulkner apparently marked up a copy (which has subsequently been lost), but abandoned the project as too expensive in those parlous economic times.[16] It was not republished in the United States until 1946, in the wake of renewed interest in Faulkner spurred by a variety of things, including Malcolm Cowley's editing of *The Portable Faulkner* (1946),[17] Robert Penn Warren's influential review of the *Portable,*[18] and Albert Camus' and Jean-Paul Sartre's important "discovery" of his books in the thirties and forties, in their French translations. In 1946 it appeared with *As I Lay Dying* in a Modern Library volume, along with the "Compson Appendix," which Faulkner had written in 1945, ostensibly as a sort of introduction to Cowley's selection from the novel's fourth section. In the mid-fifties the Modern Library and Vintage reissued the first edition text in facsimile, and this text remained in print, with the Compson Appendix, until 1984, when the present editor prepared a new text based on Faulkner's carbon typescript (for a complete record of the editing, see Polk[19]). That text, with a couple of corrections in later printings, has been used in subsequent issues of the novel, including Vintage (1987), the Norton Casebook (1987), Vintage International (1990), and the Modern Library (1992); it was issued in 1992 on computer diskette by Voyager.

The 1984 text and its subsequent issues omit the "Compson Appendix," though the new Modern Library text does include it, along with a prefatory note which explains something of its problematic relationship to the novel proper. That relationship is worth a word here. On September 20, 1945, Faulkner suggested that Malcolm Cowley include the "last section, the Dilsey one," in *The Portable Faulkner,* and proposed to write "a page or two of synopsis to preface it, a condensation of the first 3 sections, which simply told why and when (and who she was) and how a 17 year old girl robbed a bureau drawer of hoarded money and climbed down a drain pipe and ran off with a carnival pitchman."[20] Less than a month later, on October 18, he sent Cowley not a one- or two-page synopsis, but a completely new short-story-length discursive genealogy of the entire Compson clan: "I should have done this when I wrote the book," he wrote Cowley. "Then the whole thing would have fallen into pattern like a jigsaw puzzle when the magician's wand touched it.... I think it is really pretty good, to stand as it is, as a piece without implications."[21] On February 4, 1946, he was still enthusiastic about it; he wrote to Robert Linscott of Random House about a proposed new edition of the novel: "When you reprint THE SOUND AND THE FURY, I have a new section to go with it. I should have written this new section when I wrote the book itself.... By all means include this in the reprint. When you read it, you will see how it is the key to the whole book, and after reading it, the 4 sections as they stand now fall into clarity and place."[22]

All this notwithstanding the 1984 Random House edition did not include the Appendix, for reasons having to do with the editor's decision to produce a text of the novel as it would have been originally published in 1929, and with the broader context of Faulkner's life and career in the mid-1940s, as he approached his fiftieth birthday. The forties were especially difficult and bitter years for him. After the furious pace of the previous decade (he published thirteen books between 1929 and 1942), he slowed almost to a stop, partly through miserable contractual obligations with Hollywood and partly through an increasing preoccupation with *A Fable.* After 1942 he published only one new piece (the Appendix) before *Intruder in the Dust* in 1948. He had numerous personal troubles, as well as professional and artistic anxieties about the effect he feared Hollywood was having on his work, on his capacity to produce, and on his ability to make a decent living, and about the generally low esteem in which his work was held in his own country. "What a commentary," he wrote his agent Harold Ober in January 1946, upon receiving a check for winning a prize in an *Ellery Queen's Mystery Magazine* contest: "In France, I am the father of a literary movement. In Europe I am considered the best modern American and among the first of all writers. In America, I eke out a hack's motion picture wages by winning second prize in a manufactured mystery story contest."[23]

He was, then, at a very low personal and professional ebb, and it is not difficult to understand why he was so enthusiastic about the Compson Appendix. This superlative piece, a return to familiar territory after the torment of Hollywood scriptwriting and the difficulties of *A Fable*, proved to him that his powers as a writer had indeed not failed him entirely. This renewed self-confidence, along with Cowley's interest and Random House's decision to republish *The Sound and the Fury* and *As I Lay Dying* in a single Modern Library volume, surely gave him reason to be optimistic about his future. But he was still mindful of having been misunderstood and underappreciated for all of his career, and was, perhaps, uncharacteristically tender-skinned about his reputation, now apparently on the upswing, enough so to be wary of subjecting *The Sound and the Fury*, his "heart's darling," to another bout of misunderstanding. Thus in his depression over the state of his life and career, and wanting to forestall with the new edition a repetition of the misunderstanding and current neglect of the original, he saw the Appendix as somehow making the novel comprehensible and so more accessible to the reader: "As you will see," he wrote Linscott, "this appendix is the key to the whole book; after reading this, any reader will understand all the other sections. That was the trouble before," he continued: "the BENJY section, although the most obscure and troublesome one, had to come first because of chronology, the matter it told." He even wanted the Appendix to appear first, though retaining the title "Appendix": "to title this new section FOREWORD seems bad to me, as a deliberate pandering to those who wont make the effort to understand the book."[24] It is not clear how printing it at the beginning of the book as "Appendix" is less a "pandering" to those "who wont make the effort" than printing it at the beginning as a "Foreword," though perhaps the idea of having an appendix first appealed to his sense of the book's anachronological structure. The Appendix was first published in *The Portable Faulkner* in 1946, then in the Modern Library's dual edition of *The Sound and the Fury* and *As I Lay Dying* in the same year, and finally in the 1962 Vintage paperback reissue of the original 1929 text, where it appeared at the end, rather than at the beginning, of the volume. Scholars and critics and students, not aware of its complicated relationship to the 1929 text, have frequently treated it as an equal part of the novel.

In spite of Faulkner's late desires and enthusiasms, which were not completely coherent, it seems proper to consider the Appendix not as part of the novel, but rather as a separate entity, distinct from *The Sound and the Fury* in the same way that "That Evening Sun" and other stories involving the Compsons are distinct fictional entities. It may be helpful to think of the Appendix in the same way we think, for example, of Fitzgerald's postpublication revisions of *Tender Is the Night,* which represent second thoughts about a published novel that had met neither critical nor popular success in its original avatar. He revised at a time well after the original impulse had been lost, or at least altered, for reasons extraneous to the novel itself. In any case, a *Sound and Fury* that begins with the Compson Appendix is *different* from the one that begins: "Through the fence, between the curling flower spaces, I could see them hitting." – different and, in my judgment, considerably diminished from the constant rare white heat of the 1929 text, with its deliberately controlled revelation and concealment of the Compson family history, and its carefully contrived ambiguities, all of which are seriously compromised if the reader approaches them from the vantage of the Appendix; a *Sound and Fury* to which the Appendix is attached at the end, without proper bibliographical explanations, is a novel carrying baggage that has created problems for unsuspecting readers and critics. Whatever Faulkner meant when he said that the Appendix could stand alone, as a piece "without implications," it does indeed have numerous implications when attached, front or back, to the novel proper,[25] and readers should be as careful and sophisticated when reading these two related documents as when reading, say, *The Sound and the Fury* and *Absalom, Absalom!,* which are related in similar ways.

There is no way adequately to summarize the large body of writings about *The Sound and the Fury,* and so the following is intended only as the barest of outlines. It is based on, and readers are encouraged to read for themselves, several longer essays on the general history of Faulkner criticism (especially that of Hoffman and Vickery[26]), and on the annotated bibliographies provided by Bleikasten,[27] McHaney,[28] and Bassett,[29] the essay by Meriwether in *Sixteen Modern American Authors,*[30] and that by Zender, Cohen, and Krause in *Sixteen Modern American Authors Vol. 2* (1990).[31]

Good criticism of *The Sound and the Fury* began even before it was published. The novel's publisher sent galley proofs of Faulkner's novel to another of its authors, Evelyn Scott, who wrote a perceptive and enthusiastic essay, *On William Faulkner's "The Sound and the Fury,"* which was published as a separate pamphlet simultaneously with the novel.[32] Scott was the first to suggest that the novel reached the proportions of Greek tragedy. Reviews on publication were mixed, some critics responding enthusiastically to the novel's freshness and vitality; others were befuddled by the complex demand it made on readers, and decided the result just wasn't worth the effort.

With few exceptions, most commentary in the next two decades came partly in reaction to Faulkner's astonishing output – he published nine novels and two collections of stories between *The Sound and the Fury* in 1929 and *Go Down, Moses* in 1942 – and partly because of his growing reputation (mostly thanks to the horrific nature of *Sanctuary* [1931] and to his sarcastic introduction to the Modern Library issue of that novel in 1932) as a purveyor of things Southern, lurid, and exotic, and therefore as having a preoccupation with the sinister and the bizarre and the abnormal. Alan R. Thompson[33] called him the master of "the cult of cruelty," a label that managed to stick with him in one or more variations, throughout his life and well after. Granville Hicks, writing in September of 1931, was uncomfortably appreciative of Faulkner's technique, and so concluded that he was merely playing stylistic games with readers, "perversely" rearranging chronology for no particular reason. Hicks considered that Faulkner's work lacked sufficiently meaningful social and moral dimensions,[34] a common complaint among leftist critics and journalists of the thirties.

Faulkner's output subsequent to *The Sound and the Fury,* set largely in Yoknapatawpha County, made it easy – and convenient – for critics to assume that he was writing *about* the South, and to see *The Sound and the Fury* in that Southern context. George Marion O'Donnell's influential essay in 1939[35] proposed a simplistic schema that divided Faulkner's characters into Sartorises – Old South aristocrats on their way out in the modern world – and Snopeses – the conniving and amoral commercializing redneck-turned-petit bourgeois of the New South who were taking over from the defunctive Old. *The Sound and the Fury* was thus *about* the decline of a Southern family and, by extension, about the simultaneous decline of the Old South.

There were some sympathetic treatments which found other things in the work besides Southern history, and which managed to lay out ground for dealing with other aspects of theme and technique. James Burnham, in a 1931 appreciative essay called "Trying to Say," was doubtless the first to discuss the novel's concern with language, a major preoccupation of critics of the past two decades.[36] After reading Maurice-Edgar Coindreau's translation, *La bruit et la fureur* (1937), Maurice Le Breton in 1937[37] and Jean-Paul Sartre (1939)[38] wrote discerning essays. Sartre's is an especially important and influential essay, discussing Faulkner's use of time in *The Sound and the Fury.* He contended that Faulkner was a better fiction writer than metaphysician, since his characters, locked in their pasts, had no future in which to be free. Coindreau's introduction to his translation is an important discussion of the problems of translating such a novel; it also contains some interesting biographical information, gleaned from his interviews with Faulkner as he translated.

Not surprisingly, novelists and poets have generally been extremely sympathetic with and receptive to Faulkner's work. Conrad Aiken in 1939[39] and Warren Beck in 1941[40] wrote perceptive essays on Faulkner's style, essays which took Faulkner seriously as an artist, and both implicitly and explicitly rejected the prevailing judgments that he wrote hastily and carelessly – a charge heard with increasing frequency after Faulkner's 1932 introduction to the Modern Library *Sanctuary* and prompted by the astonishing frequency with which his novels and stories appeared. As Beck put it: "Faulkner is neither mysterious nor monstrous, he is not arcane nor remote, he is merely prodigious in every sense." Both writers included sensible comments on *The Sound and the Fury* in essays otherwise general in their nature.

Serious scholarly and academic writing about *The Sound and the Fury* began in the years following World War II, and matured during the fifties in a rash of articles and chapters in books. They dealt with a variety of its distinctive elements – its sources in and indebtedness to Shakespeare, Freud, Eliot, Joyce, and other writers of the early twentieth century. Critics were interested in the novel's narrative technique, its use of the stream of consciousness, and its Christian symbolism. Four essays in Alan Downer's 1954 collection, *English Institute Essays 1952,*[41] have continued to be of interest: Cleanth Brooks's "Primitivism in *The Sound and the Fury*" argues that Faulkner did not valorize primitive, natural, instinctual behavior in his characters, but rather insisted that they deal sophisticatedly with life's moral complexities. In his still controversial "The Interior Monologues of *The Sound and the Fury,*" Carvel Collins suggested several of the novel's debts to Shakespeare and Joyce and argued that as Joyce had structured *Ulysses* upon *The Odyssey,* Faulkner built his novel around Freud's tri-partite structure of the personality; in this structure, Benjy is roughly equivalent to the id, Quentin to the ego, and Jason the superego. Perrin Lowrey's "Concepts of Time in *The Sound and the Fury*" argued that there was more than one concept of time in the novel, and Lawrance R. Thompson's "Mirror Analogues in *The Sound and the Fury*" suggested that mirror imagery in the novel was directly related to the novel's overall structure. Also in 1954 Olga W. Vickery's "*The Sound and the Fury:* A Study in Perspective" appeared in *PMLA;* this essay, slightly revised for republication in her later *The Novels of William Faulkner* (1959; rev. 1964),[42] is perhaps the first really important discussion of the novel's overall structure, the interrelatedness of all its component parts, and is still very much worth consulting. Michel Gresset's "Psychological Aspects of Evil in *The*

Sound and the Fury" (1966)[43] is a very useful discussion of a dominant theme.

Still the most useful and influential studies of the novel's overall design and significance are those of Brooks, in *The Yoknapatawpha Country* (1963),[44] and Michael Millgate, whose chapter in *The Achievement of William Faulkner* (1966)[45] was the first to demonstrate how valuable to an understanding of the novel were the author's manuscripts and typescripts, which were then becoming available for study at their permanent home at the University of Virginia. Edmond L. Volpe's chapter in *A Reader's Guide to William Faulkner* (1964)[46] is also very helpful both as a general commentary on the novel's various meanings and as a guide to the intricacies of its chronological structure. Perhaps the best study of a single character in the novel is Eileen Gregory's "Caddy Compson's World" (1970).[47] Stephen M. Ross's "The 'Loud World' of Quentin Compson" (1975)[48] is an excellent study of voice in the novel. François L. Pitavy's "Through the Poet's Eye: A View of Quentin Compson" (1975)[49] also has some very interesting things to say about voice.

Modern criticism of *The Sound and the Fury* begins in the mid-1970s, with John T. Irwin's *Doubling and Incest/Repetition and Revenge: A Speculative Reading of Faulkner* (1975)[50] and André Bleikasten's *"The Most Splendid Failure"* (1976).[51] Both books draw upon an extraordinary number of textual and extratextual sources to help illuminate the murkier corners of *The Sound and the Fury.* Irwin's is a rousing structuralist and psychoanalytic reading of the interstices between *The Sound and the Fury* and *Absalom, Absalom!* and others of Faulkner's novels, which focuses on the oedipal struggle between father and son. Bleikasten's book asks new questions about the novel, and not so much in the answering as in the meditations on the questions offers excellent insights into traditional critical concerns like character and narrative and theme; but it also lays out new ways of thinking about the novel's language, its sources in the author's psyche, and its relationship to Faulkner's other books, which later critics have responded to. Both books remain central in *The Sound and the Fury* criticism, touchstones to which most subsequent criticism pays its respects even when disagreeing or moving beyond them. Other recent work very much worth consulting for some sense of the current trend in criticism of the novel are the chapters in John T. Matthews' *The Play of Faulkner's Language* (1983),[52] Donald M. Kartiganer's *The Fragile Thread: The Meaning of Form in Faulkner's Novels* (1979),[53] and Minrose Gwin's feminist reading in her *The Feminine and Faulkner: Reading (Beyond) Sexual Difference* (1990).[54] My own *An Editorial Handbook* (1985)[55] provides the rationale for editorial choices made in preparing the *New Corrected Edition* of *The Sound and the Fury* published in 1984.

The essays in this volume expand on the present state of things in useful ways. Dawn Trouard offers us the women of *The Sound and the Fury* as we have not seen them before. Reading against the grain of the predominant critical tradition which sees them through the lens of masculine cultural biases, she insists that the women are very much *in* the text, and that the tradition's emphasis on Caddy – even that, especially that, which wants to make her the center of the novel, albeit an absent one – has effectively reduced her and the other female characters to monolithic, singular figures who exist only to cause, or at least take the blame for, male suffering. Seeing the novel through Luce Irigaray's *This Sex Which Is Not One*, Trouard raises disturbing questions about how we have read the novel, and shows us a group of women who are much more various and complex than we have thus far seen. In an especially rich appendix to her essay which focuses on Melissa Meek, the librarian of the Compson Appendix of 1946, Trouard makes us more fully aware of Meek's and the Appendix's complex and intimate, and quite moving, relationship with the original novel.

Donald M. Kartiganer comes to terms with the ways in which *The Sound and the Fury* simultaneously attracts readers and resists *readings*. The novel insists, he claims, on "clinging to the letter of its borrowed title" and so on "signifying nothing." It carries its resistance to being read "to the most extreme end this side of incoherence, in the sense that it seems to withstand from beginning to end every critical strategy." According to Kartiganer, part of Faulkner's technique in the novel is to inscribe directly into it not just, following Joyce in *Ulysses*, a variety of writing styles, but also a variety of reading and critical strategies, which it parodies by including and so co-opting them. Each brother's first-person narration is a parody of twentieth-century literary styles and techniques – Benjy is the Imagist voice, Quentin the voice of High Modernism, Jason that of Postmodernism – which build on, but finally explode, the possibilities for comprehension that each seems to offer. The fourth section, often identified as "Faulkner's" section, does nothing to "reconcile the novel's differing perspectives," even though, unlike the first three sections, it seems to offer us a more traditional fictional technique, "a fictional mode grounded on the assumption of coherent and significant ending." It is nevertheless of a piece with the brothers' narratives: it is "the fourth mystification" which "lifts the depiction of 'reality' itself to the level of original invention, overcoming its own strict referentiality, its seemingly faithful account of the truth of the world, and establishing itself as one more re-creation of the Compson story."

Richard Godden's contribution is a closely argued discussion of the relationship between incest and miscegenation. By pointing out the intricate web of associations between the language of blackness and each brother's preoccupation with Caddy's body, Godden insists that the relationship of turn-of-the-century racial myths to the incest dream is a preoccupation with incest not as Freudian psychological nightmare, but as a product of political and sociological, cultural, forces. What the brothers share "is not attributable to a universal psychology (Freudian or otherwise) but to an historically specific regional pathology." Godden's placement of Quentin's remove to Cambridge against the specific historical context offers us rich readings of such characters as the remarkable Deacon and the little Italian girl who accompanies Quentin through part of his journey on his final day.

My own contribution looks very closely at the ways the smallest units of the novel function together – the word, the punctuation, the syntax – and demonstrates just how radical, and how successful, Faulkner's experiments with language, the whole notion of "trying to say," were. In *The Sound and the Fury,* Faulkner faces the problematics of the representation of language on paper, and makes that problem part of the novel's thematic understructure. He forces us as readers to come to terms with the representation of language by making us deal with those mechanics – punctuation, spelling, and paragraphing, not to say grammatical structure – as part of the language itself. Thus the written representation of the novel's putatively oral monologues – those of the three brothers and of the Reverend Shegog in the fourth section – often works to reveal to readers things that these "narrators" would very much like to keep hidden, even from themselves.

NOTES

1 "Introduction" to *The Sound and the Fury*. In André Bleikasten, ed., *William Faulkner's The Sound and the Fury: A Critical Casebook* (New York: Garland, 1982), pp. 9–10.
2 James B. Meriwether and Michael Millgate, eds., *Lion in the Garden: Interviews with William Faulkner 1926–1962* (New York: Random House, 1968), p. 245.
3 *Lion in the Garden*, p. 146.
4 "Introduction," p. 14.
5 Joseph Blotner and Frederick L. Gwynn, eds. *Faulkner in the University* (New York: Vintage, 1965), p. 77.
6 James G. Watson, ed. *Thinking of Home: William Faulkner's Letters to His Mother and Father 1918–1925*. (New York: Norton, 1992), pp. 29–65.
7 Collins, "Biographical Background for Faulkner's *Helen*." In *Helen: A Courtship and Mississippi Poems* (New Orleans and Oxford: Tulane University and the Yoknapatawpha Press), 1981, pp. 29, 99n.16.
8 Faulkner wrote *Sanctuary* in 1929, but did not publish it until 1931 in a version that he had heavily revised in galleys. The original version, not published until 1981, demonstrates closer affinities to *Flags* than the revised text. See Polk, "Afterword" to *Sanctuary: The Original Text* (New York: Random House, 1981).
9 Polk, "Afterword," p. 299.
10 Joseph Blotner, ed., *Selected Letters of William Faulkner* (New York: Random House, 1977), p. 17.
11 Ben Wasson, *Count No 'Count: Flashbacks to Faulkner* (Jackson: University Press of Mississippi, 1983), p. 89.
12 Joseph Blotner, *Faulkner: A Biography*. 2 vols. (New York: Random House, 1974), vol. 1, p. 602.
13 Noel Polk, *An Editorial Handbook for William Faulkner's The Sound and the Fury* (New York: Garland, 1985). See Appendix C.

14 *Selected Letters,* pp. 44–6.
15 *Selected Letters,* pp. 44–5.
16 Blotner, *Faulkner: A Biography,* vol. 1, pp. 793, 805.
17 New York: Viking.
18 Robert Penn Warren, "Cowley's Faulkner." *New Republic,* August 12, 1946: 176–80; August 26, 1946: 234–7. Reprinted in Frederick W. Hoffman, and Olga Vickery, eds., *Three Decades of Faulkner Criticism* (New York: Harcourt, Brace & World, 1963), pp. 109–24.
19 Most of the discussion in this essay is drawn directly from my introduction to the *Editorial Handbook.*
20 *Selected Letters,* p. 202.
21 Ibid., p. 205.
22 Ibid., p. 220.
23 Ibid., pp. 217–18.
24 Ibid., p. 228.
25 See the useful discussion by Mary Jane Dickerson, " 'The Magician's Wand': Faulkner's Compson Appendix," *Mississippi Quarterly,* 28 (Summer 1975): 317–37.
26 *Three Decades of Criticism,* pp. 1–50.
27 Bleikasten, *Casebook,* pp. 155–69.
28 Thomas L. McHaney, *William Faulkner: A Reference Guide* (Boston: G. K. Hall, 1976).
29 John Bassett, *William Faulkner: An Annotated Checklist of Criticism* (New York: David Lewis, 1972).
30 James B. Meriwether, "William Faulkner," in Jackson R. Bryer, ed., *Sixteen Modern American Authors* (Durham: Duke University Press, 1969; revised and updated 1973), pp. 223–75.
31 Karl Zender, Philip Cohen, and David Krause, "William Faulkner," in Bryer, *Sixteen Modern American Authors, vol. 2.*
32 New York: Jonathan Cape and Harrison Smith, 1929. In Arthur Kinney ed., *Critical Essays on William Faulkner: The Compson Family* (Boston: G. K. Hall, 1982), pp. 115–18.
33 Alan R. Thompson, "The Cult of Cruelty," *Bookman* 74 (January–February 1932): 477–87.
34 Granville Hicks, "The Past and Future of William Faulkner," *Bookman* 74 (September 1931): 17–24.
35 George Marion O'Donnell, "Faulkner's Mythology," *Kenyon Review* 1 (Summer 1939): 258–99. In Hoffman and Vickery.
36 James Burnham, "Trying to Say," *Symposium* 2 (January 1931): 51–9.
37 Maurice le Breton, "Technique et psychologie chez William Faulkner," *Études Anglaises* 1 (September 1937): 418–38.

38 Jean-Paul Sartre, "A propos de 'Le Bruit et la Fureur': la temporalité chez Faulkner," *Nouvelle revue française* 52 (June 1940): 1057–61; 53 (July): 147–51. In Hoffman and Vickery.

39 Conrad Aiken, "William Faulkner: The Novel as Form," *Atlantic Monthly* 144 (November 1939): 650–4. In Hoffman and Vickery.

40 Warren Beck, "William Faulkner's Style," *American Prefaces* (Spring 1941): 195–211. In Hoffman and Vickery.

41 Alan S. Downer, ed., *English Institute Essays 1952* (New York: Columbia University Press, 1954).

42 Olga W. Vickery, "*The Sound and the Fury:* A Study in Perspective" in Vickery, *The Novels of William Faulkner: A Critical Interpretation* (Baton Rouge: Louisiana State University Press, 1959; rev. 1964), pp. 28–49.

43 Michel Gresset, "Psychological Aspects of Evil in *The Sound and the Fury*," *Mississippi Quarterly* 19 (Summer 1966): 143–53.

44 New Haven: Yale University Press.

45 New York: Random House.

46 New York: Noonday Press.

47 Eileen Gregory, "Caddy Compson's World," in *The Merrill Studies in The Sound and the Fury* (Columbus, Ohio: Charles E. Merrill, 1970), pp. 89–101.

48 Stephen M. Ross, "The 'Loud World' of Quentin Compson." *Studies in the Novel* 7 (Summer 1975): 245–57. Reprinted in Bleikasten, *Casebook*, pp. 101–14.

49 François Pitavy, "Through the Poet's Eye: A View of Quentin Compson," in Bleikasten, *Casebook*, pp. 79–99.

50 Baltimore: Johns Hopkins University Press.

51 Bloomington: Indiana University Press.

52 "The Discovery of Loss in *The Sound and the Fury*," in *The Play of Faulkner's Language* (Ithaca: Cornell University Press, 1982), pp. 63–114.

53 Amherst: University of Massachusetts Press, 1979, pp. 3–22.

54 "Hearing Caddy's Voice," in *The Feminine and Faulkner: Reading (Beyond) Sexual Difference* (Knoxville: University of Tennessee Press, 1990), pp. 34–62.

55 Polk, *Editorial Handbook*.

2

Faulkner's Text Which Is Not One

DAWN TROUARD

IN ITS SIXTY years of public life, *The Sound and the Fury* has inspired different degrees of enthusiasm. From early assessments that judged it "a trifle unhealthy"[1] to others that found it "downright tiresome,"[2] it has managed to remain, even in these days of canon cross fire, in the expropriated words of Faulkner, "our heart's darling" – a book "we" love to teach.[3] To write about it in 1992 is to confront the critical monolith, made worse now because there seems little left unsaid about a work that properly, intentionally, and "officially" failed.[4] Even the book's own designated heart's darling, Caddy herself, has endured a contested critical history: she has been both examined as the source of Compson ruin and elevated to the status of "the beautiful one." Each critical construction of her has been replicated many times over. Faulkner's decision to deny her a narrative voice has worked to spawn dozens of apologias which seek to demonstrate that her absence is central, *central* to the novel, central to the brothers' lives and memories, central to the structural strategy of the work, central to its rhetoricized tragedy,[5] central even to the fall of the South.[6] Faulkner aided and abetted this compelling interpretation when he claimed to have written the book to appease his haunted desire for a sister that never was, for the daughter he lost, and who – in the ritualized telling – became the metaphorically beautiful urn which in turn became, finally, something to die for or with. Scholars of *The Sound and the Fury* have stood faithful vigil, invoking Faulkner's variations on the creed. In most essays on the work there is the near-obligatory Caddy who is brave, the Quentin who loved some concept of Compson honor, the Mr. Compson who reminds us that no Compson ever disappointed a lady, and the bellowing, ricklickshun, doomed, damned, first and de last. They [the critics] endure, offering fellow Faulknerians extraordinary and comforting consensus about the Compson boys, Caddy's energy, and Dilsey's strength, along with breathtakingly unanimous assessments of Mrs. Compson, who has served faithfully as the Rotten Mother for critics to rail against. The mystique that surrounds certain elements of the book's genesis – the muddy seat of a little girl's drawers – and some maxims about the book's message are at least partly responsible for its canonical status. Eric J. Sundquist calls Faulkner's story about the novel's inception the "genetic myth" that has "overwhelmed the novel itself";[7] and he has gone on to charge quite heretically that the novel "offers few philosophical ideas of lasting concern."[8] But even if its ideas are not lasting, the critics' concern with them certainly has been.[9] Certain views on the novel have been reworked so frequently that they have become virtual articles of faith that direct our readings and preempt substantive controversy.

The critical fetishizing of despair has produced an aesthetic affirmation that keeps the book on the academy's hit parade. Yet, in so relentlessly unifying *The Sound and the Fury* around traditional expectations for tragedy and standards of modernism, critics have done it a disservice: by homogenizing its complexity and sidestepping its discrepancies, they have undermined Faulkner's intentions. Rather than enabling Faulkner to slam the door to the publishers' addresses and book lists, academic institutionalization of *The Sound and the Fury* has guaranteed that Faulkner would show up semester after semester on reading lists everywhere. We have rewarded his daring by impressing the book that cost him "the most grief" into the service of a cultural status quo.[10] Regularly drafted to shore up the beatitudes, *The Sound and the Fury* has permitted academic champions of truth and beauty to find overriding coherence and enduring truth in the very structures Faulkner dreamed would thwart bourgeois convention.

In this essay, I should like to tamper particularly with another of the critical myths that have overwhelmed *The Sound and the Fury,* the fiercely defended notion of the book's coherence, or at least of a coherence accomplished through an unshakable faith in Caddy's centrality and unity. To challenge the book's status as unified text and to focus attention on a plot overshadowed by the culturally privileged saga of sons, I intend to reframe each narrative section and search out discrepancies and ruptures in the depiction of the Compson women who shuttle in and out of the sections waiting to be summoned from the textual perimeters for service in the male symbolic. Because so many of the book's stories interlock, my method is irresistibly recursive; but since my task is re-vision, I need to pursue differences in conception and emphasis in the representation of the Compson mothers and daughters. By unearthing the stories grounded in the work's record of female experience, I can explore the ways the mother-daughter plots subvert cherished assumptions about the unity of the work. I have chosen to reclaim each of the units for a different Compson woman; I have imagined for each of the sections a day which reflects a woman's stake in the narrative. By recognizing the pervasive presence and importance of the Compson women, I hope to highlight the traditional resistance to their integration, and to stake out actual fictional territory for them: Benjy's "Good Friday" will become Caroline Compson's "Mother's Day."[11]

In the reclamation project, I hope to allow us to see again, or for the first time, Caddy of the muddy drawers, Benjy's Caddy, who has been so critically enshrined in the readings of the work that she has become inseparable from the Caddy breathing o'er Eden, Quentin's Caddy. And Quentin's Caddy, who was "always a king or a giant or a general,"[12] has inevitably and naturally merged with Jason's Caddy in section three, where she is powerless, at his mercy, futilely pleading with him to be kind to her child. The defiant little girl, braver than the brothers and cherished by the critics, bears little resemblance to *this* woman, also known as Caddy. By "April Eighth" a/k/a section four a/k/a Easter Sunday 1928, Caddy has been so radically metamorphosed that she exists only as provocative and tortured sound. Progressively destroyed in each successive representation in the 1929 text, she completes the negative spiral of a woman who has tragically failed everyone, however inadvertently. To view Caddy as a unified, single figure, as the criticism has done, distorts, even erases, in practice and spirit, possibilities for understanding Caddy and the complexities of female experience. Each of *The Sound and the Fury*'s varied representations of Caddy's departures, disappearances, or removals from the Compson household has led readers to improvise a coherent and unified Caddy that coherently explains Benjy's bellowing, Jason's rage, Quentin's suicide, and the bleakness of the final section. Close attention to the distinct Caddy in each separate section reveals that her whereabouts are strictly unaccounted for; she does not add up; she can't be reconciled – she is more than one. Caddy has been understood as a sister who climbs a tree, who becomes unvirgin, or who is once and always a bitch. But understanding this depends on a logic supplied by the reader that the text does not bear out. Readers have found it easier to believe in a Caddy "somewhere" brave, doomed, and beautiful than to confront the contradictions her character embodies. Conditioned to recognize her as familiar, readers, with Benjy, bellow at her invocation and continue to believe she smells like trees, even when she is redolent of honeysuckle and rain, even when she smells like nothing at all.

That readers have not been troubled by highly discrepant versions of her behavior and unaccounted for changes in her character underscores how thoroughly our attention has been diverted by the male rhetoric that fills the space vacated by the perpetually and variously absent Caddys. For all the attention we have paid to *Caddy,* we have barely seen her. We recognize her only because we have helped make her, colluding in the construction of her as a beautiful little girl *cum* urn. This transformation of girl into urn – an apotheosis of art transcending loss – accomplishes a distortion that Luce Irigaray sees as the necessary *"blurring"* of females in order to produce the *same,* which is the unified idealism demanded by patriarchal culture.[13] By rendering the different versions of Caddy the *same,* readers have both thematically and technically fostered a specious sense of the book's coherence. Convinced of its "oneness," readers have suppressed considerations that are incompatible with the dominant mythology, readings that might significantly "jam the machinery" of the ideal hegemonic readings designed to secure allegiance to unity and systematicity.[14] We have been complicit far too long in reproducing *The Sound and the Fury* as a monument to high modernism, a sacred text unifying and celebrating a male despair rooted in and at the expense of female difference.

Prevailing myths of *The Sound and the Fury* have enshrined Caddy in a kind of death in life, justified her silence, and stamped her as doomed, isolated out of the loud and vital world of possibility. My resistance to a single Caddy is not a fanatical de-essentialism. I do not think she has been merely altered by the years, real and imaginative, separating her from Faulkner's original inception. Though Faulkner used this claim himself to account for Caddy's differences when he dodged queries about factual discrepancies in the work, I think there is more to be gained by refusing his claims of increasing familiarity, that he simply knew her better by the time of the Appendix than he did in 1929.[15] Rather, I'd like to argue that Caddy never has been one. Existing in fluid subversion, flowing between and around and even against the accounts of her that attempt to contain and unify her, the contradictory Caddys resist finality, closure, and coherence. Our need to see her as one, with a past and a certain negotiable value in an economy based in the masculine imaginary, tells us a lot about how we deny alternatives and challenges to female experience that threaten the prescriptive authority of the masculine imaginary.

Suppose Caddy is present in a variety of her contradictions, different and untranscendent in each of the sections, and that she is not the only woman who is more than merely one. Suppose Faulkner employed the Compson women with no regard to the rules of the novel and character as he knew it. What happens if we see Mrs. Compson as both good mother *and* selfish woman, and Quentin, her granddaughter, both as victim and freedom fighter? Compelled to reconcile, legitimate, and *make sense,* we have captured Faulkner's characters in readings that struggle to make his art consistent, to make his characters cast shadows. As a result we find familiar motivations, discover consistencies where none may exist, where none were perhaps intended to exist. Not unlike Joe Christmas, we have managed to arrive always at our point of departure with *The Sound and the Fury;* looking up Caddy's dress for the answer, we have found the story of the two lost women that Faulkner told us was there. We have irresistibly and inevitably ended by reporting the story that accompanies – rather displaces – all other stories: the story of exquisite and valorized male suffering, the story of men, men moaning, men forced to buy flatirons and finish the term at Harvard, and men standing in poison ivy. We dismiss inconsistent data contravening the official and familiar sense of the characters and surrender ourselves to what we have convinced ourselves they ought to be saying and doing.[16] We sacrifice complexity to the aesthetic need to see both Caddy and her "novel" as something *to die for.*

And so I propose a variation on Mr. Compson's Thoreauvian advice to Quentin that he take an econo-vacation in Maine and defer suicide. My excursion for recovery's sake launches us toward Irigaray's exteriority, the realm beyond the male imaginary.[17] By upsetting arrangements and emphases that have privileged formal coherence and thematics of loss, I hope to plumb some eddies of female disruption within the sections of the 1929 edition and the Appendix, and ask some different questions. By mapping these disruptions in Faulkner's own constructed territories, I hope to locate some Caddys and Mrs. Compsons and Quentins different from the ones we have assumed were authorized. Faulkner, as owner and proprietor, set the boundaries of his familiar "somewhere," but I would like to explore its "elsewhere," the out-of-bounds, where the branch that sweeps Caddy away really begins.

If we devote some time to the relations of mothers and daughters in the work, not as a tale ancillary to the mother/son drama, we enable feminist readers and critics to begin the work, or play, of attending to female experience. The failure to consider the complex mother-daughter relationships in *The Sound and the Fury* has effectively nullified motherhood and daughterhood as values.[18] Only when we recognize the methods by which mothering in all its dimensions has been "charged" and "*turned against*" women,[19] can we hope to resist the limitations inherent in the idealized concept of a "heart's darling." The critical assumptions governing these readings offer stunning and instructive examples of how patriarchy works to preserve its values and guarantee its authority. Adrienne Rich marks the cost, the specific price of this practice, noting that "The loss of the daughter to the mother, the mother to the daughter, is the essential female tragedy."[20] Bewitched, we persist in neglecting the powerful corollary of Quentin's lament: We never ask what it would mean if Caddy could say "Mother. Mother" (95). And if ever there were a book about lost daughters, surely it is this one. If Rich is correct, and I believe she is, the "cathexis between mother and daughter – essential, distorted, misused – is the great unwritten story" (226).[21] Faulkner's mothers and daughters suffer their own tragedies in the course of the sections, and in the Appendix, and were we to analyze the elements of *female* loss and contradiction in *The Sound and the Fury,* we might accomplish the drawing, "the picture of Caddy," Faulkner was after in his many "attempts." To read *The Sound and the Fury* with a mind to find out what it really says – and doesn't say – about women may reveal it to be an even greater "son of a bitch" than we have dreamed:[22] *It is not just Caddy who "must do things for women's reasons too"* (92). In the spirit of difference I offer a working title for this excursion, *Twilight, Other Stories, and an Appendix.*[23]

Sunday, May 14, 1928 [Mother's Day]

> "I hears de wailin of women en
> de evenin lamentations" (296)

Caroline Compson is merely a complaint repeated and repeated. With the exception of Jason, no character in *The Sound and the Fury* has inspired such consensus. Synonymous with "the dungeon itself,"[24] she has been blamed by demonizers from Miss Rosa's School for Critics for the destruction of "Caddy's humanity,"[25] and even for Quentin's "refusal to conceive."[26] Dubbing her the "villain," "repressive and punitive,"[27] Linda Wagner has said that as "a mother, Caroline Compson is a complete failure."[28] Her behavior has been diagnosed as "pathogenic,"[29] and her "failure" and "maudlin egocentricity" have led to the "decay and disintegration of the Compsons."[30] Her children in their suicides, mental incapacities, and disgraces are all judgments on her, and her refrain, "I wont be around much longer," claws at the psyche of a post-Freudian and mother-hating readership: she can't – and won't – be dead soon enough. The roots of Caroline Compson's despair have not interested critics nearly so much as the trial her "hypochondria" has been for the Compson family; in almost every appearance in the 1929 text, she grotesquely provides the ammunition of self-hatred, and critics have compliantly pummeled her for self-absorption, cruelty, and sanctimoniousness. She has become, at least critically, in fact, a monster,[31] the mother of all our nightmares.

Caroline Compson comes to us most immediately through the three 1928 narratives that present her as a widow and the financially strapped sister of an alcoholic and derelict brother. She is also the mother of a suicide, an idiot son, and a clerk ensconced at the town store. She is finally a grandmother. Faulkner provides all the space necessary to recognize the woman drawn in "That Evening Sun," a woman who believed "that all day father had been trying to think of doing the thing she wouldn't like the most, and that she knew all the time that after a while he would think of it."[32] In the absence of any details about her past, Mrs. Compson is perhaps harder than usual to imagine as a woman who was at once bride and new mother. But if we cannot believe in some version of her that is "attractive" and potentially maternal, we have more questions to ask about Mr. Compson's perversity than the occasion of this reading will permit me to consider. Granting that life has depleted her resources, and conceding that by 1928 she is broken, inept, and pathetic, should we not still ask whether the Mrs. Compson we have remembered is the Mrs. Compson that was always? The text offers no clues to the elements that gradually or suddenly produced the figure of a woman who calls and complains from the confines of her room and whom Quentin has suspected of watching him malignantly. We do not have her version of things any more than we have Caddy's or Miss Quentin's.

We know from section one that she dreads Christmas and has always felt socially inferior as a Bascomb to the Compson line of generals and governors. The magnitude of her misery in the Compson domain is epic. She pleads with her husband to let her take Jason and go away (100–3). Her fears of marginality, which ought to prove her petty paranoia, perceived as just another occasion for her to chide, become curiously prophetic when we discover that she is largely excluded from family history in the 1946 Appendix. Mentioned only for renaming Benjy and discovering his castration too late to prevent it (344), she warrants mention for her dying, which in turn is the key to Jason's infamous racist joke: 1933 marks for Jason not so much his mother's death as the year when he is "freed from the niggers" (345). Caroline Compson as an individual in the Compson genealogy occupies barely two clauses; even Ikkemotubbe and Andrew Jackson are granted more space and interpretive history. We can only speculate whether Caroline Compson, like Maud, Faulkner's own mother, imagined a heaven where she would not have to suffer conversation with the husband she had survived by twenty years, and never liked.[33]

Evidence for other possible readings of Caroline Compson exists in the text proper, but it has usually been marshaled against her or even erased. A much cited episode in section one preserves Mrs. Compson fretfully in the act of overseeing Caddy and Benjy's preparation for an outing. In this scene, Caddy has traditionally been viewed as the caring one, intervening for Benjy against Mrs. Compson's desire to keep him inside. When Mrs. Compson exclaims "My poor baby," critics leap to prefer Caddy's attitude: "You're not a poor baby. Are you. Are you. You've got your Caddy. Haven't you got your Caddy" (8–9). Mrs. Compson, in the same scene, has been faulted for asking whether Benjy is cold rather than checking him herself. Her admonitions to Caddy not to lift Benjy lest she hurt her "carriage" and that it is vital for her to learn to *think* for Benjy and herself (8) have also been seen as more evidence of Mrs. Compson's monstrousness. In fact, Caddy, who seems very eager to be out of the house, has started to take Benjy out without shoes, and Mrs. Compson has responsibly intervened. She not only asks Caddy to "take good care of him," calling Caddy "honey," but she hugs and kisses Benjy. Efforts to berate Mrs. Compson for impaired maternal skills have led most readers to overlook Dilsey's far more brutal and critical assessment of Benjy. In the scene juxtaposed to this one, Dilsey balks at any suggestion of Benjy as anyone's "baby": "You calling that thing a baby.... A man big as T.P." (9). Mrs. Compson's style of mothering, though cloying, is nonetheless interactive, aware. Yet we have faulted her for both indifference to her children and monstrous intrusiveness. Even her caution to Caddy not to strain herself by lifting a heavy younger brother has served as evidence of her failed maternal instinct.

It is harder to defend the Mrs. Compson who has both spied on Caddy and sent Jason to do so. She has kept her discoveries from Mr. Compson; she has even theatrically donned mourning for a solid day when the fifteen-year-old Caddy has been caught kissing a boy (230). Like so many Faulkner women, she is eager to discover sin and particularly eager to monitor her daughter's chastity. Readers of the work have recoiled from the psychological brutality in Mrs. Compson's prohibition against the use of Caddy's name in the household as a condition for raising Quentin (31). Her exaggerated posturing and mock mourning make this woman who mandates this prohibition seem less consonant with the one who orchestrates a trip to French Lick to catch a husband to legitimate Caddy's pregnancy, and who also goes on to play mother-of-the-bride to a coquettish hilt during Herbert Head's visit to the family. At the very least, Quentin's section preserves a mother working very hard to get Caddy married, one nearly galvanized by the prospect of disgrace should Herbert get away. She conspires with, or for, Caddy and the granddaughter-to-be, in order to secure Herbert Head and his wealth. Uttering all the clichés of feminine hospitality and flattery, this mother-in-law as belle bears little resemblance to the woman who reportedly watches from a window, the woman unable to bear it. In fact, this Mrs. Compson plays out the scripts imposed by male fantasy (134): "You needn't be jealous though it's just an old woman he's flattering" or "Unless I do what I am tempted to and take you instead I dont think Mr Compson could overtake the car" (95); if her script is grotesque, she has only accommodated the demands for masquerade required by the patriarchal economy. Valued by the solid economy only for maternal qualities and "femininity," women, according to Irigaray, lose themselves and keep their own desires mute: "chosen as an object of consumption or of desire" women are expected to make whatever *efforts* are required to achieve the roles and images necessary to support the "infrastructure."[34] The masquerade manifests itself as a perversion of female desire. Mrs. Compson devotes all her energy to making the match work. Punishing Caddy for her pregnancy is not even a remote consideration. In her efforts to accomplish the marriage, she observes all the feminine behaviors she hopes will please her daughter's suitor. She is a different women in capability and conception. The scene tells another part of the mother-daughter story, and it is only one of the possible stories nascent and implicit in the several sections.

Only through Jason's account do we learn of the capricious and punitive Mrs. Compson. His version, however, has shaped our sense of the character more powerfully than the others. Readers compelled to see her as a villain have failed to ask why the divorce from Herbert Head would precipitate such fatal resolution in her dealings with Caddy, or even why a woman who has exercised her power primarily through illness would succeed in persuading Mr. Compson to consent to these harsh terms for his daughter? And why, of all the requests Mrs. Compson seems to have made of Mr. Compson, is this the one he acquiesces to? Where is the Mr. Compson whom Caddy reminds Jason of, the one she wouldn't "have to ask . . . twice? once, even" to take care of Quentin (209). We know neither the how nor the why of Mrs. Compson's machinations to enforce the banishment, or, in fact, even the "if." Her actions in this section highlight other significant mysteries. Why, for instance, having discovered in 1910 her power to dictate the terms of her world, does Caroline Compson devote her remaining years to a petty tyranny over Dilsey and to ongoing squabbles with Jason about how to rear Quentin? Jason reminds her that the impression the school has of her as a disciplinarian is correct: she is unable to control Quentin and apparently "never tried to do anything with her" (180). Nothing in the text provides a plausible reconciliation of the character as she was and as she now seems to have become. Though the text reveals much, it does not provide compelling explanation for why the mother denies her daughter access to the daughter's own child. Does Mrs. Compson truly believe she is doing it for Quentin's sake, or for Jason's, or is it "what she owes" to her husband's memory (220)? The explanation we have comes to us through Jason's account and through the vague reference made by Dilsey to Roskus in section one. Though she opposes the prohibition against Caddy, Dilsey does not clarify how Mrs. Compson has prevailed, nor why she,

Caddy, and Mr. Compson have not offered greater resistance to or subversion of the policy. Only Jason, who clearly profits, exhibits clear motivation and detail about how Caddy is thwarted. It is an interesting anomaly that though Jason's own track record for success is generally poor, he has nevertheless managed to keep all the women checkmated for seventeen years through his dubious cunning. The critical view that permits the paradox of Jason as devious tormentor and inept buffoon achieves similar negative capability in the sanguine construction of Mrs. Compson who at one moment is rigid and banishing, and simultaneously feckless and pathetic, duped into ritually burning her daughter's support checks. Though Mrs. Compson has calculatingly planned to acquire benefits for all the children through Caddy's advantageous marriage, she has reduced this dream to a mere hope for child support when Mr. Compson returns with Caddy's child, and she is unable to leverage even this. Mr. Compson not only has not forced the issue of child support with Herbert, but when reminded by Mrs. Compson that the law would require it, he manages to thwart her. Despite this evidence of entirely contested household power, Mrs. Compson ostensibly has the force to keep Caddy away for seventeen years though she is simultaneously undone by noise, whines for a hot water bottle, is afraid to ride in the carriage without Roskus. Expressed as a desire for Quentin to be raised without the pernicious influence of her mother, Mrs. Compson's interdiction keeps Caddy from the house with a Nietzschean resolve. Further, Mr. Compson's compliance with his wife's wishes and Caddy's overall capitulation deepen the inconsistency of characterizations in the work.

Though Mrs. Compson goes to the gravesites of her husband and son on a regular basis, she has proved less interesting to critics in her devotion than in her role as harridan, carping at Dilsey over who will drive her carriage on these excursions. In fact, the trips have been largely viewed as exercises in tormenting Dilsey and proofs of Dilsey's compassion and patience in dealing with the neurotic and demanding Mrs. Compson. That Caroline Compson's life has been circumscribed, with few possibilities for expression, scripted as mother and widow, is less a consideration than how she has monstrously deployed such scripts in her own self-interest.

Nor has it pleased critics to ponder either why so few voices from the town are heard from in this work, or why the ones who are heard invariably sympathize with Mrs. Compson. Earl, for instance, regards Mrs. Compson with respect, and feels she "has had a misfortunate life too" (229): "If it hadn't been for your mother. ... She's a lady I've got a lot of sympathy for.... Too bad some other folks I know cant say as much" (227). He reminds Jason that his "mother knows she can depend on me" (235). Even the sheriff who takes the robbery report from Jason seems to know a different Caroline than her critics have been willing to concede: "Did your mother know you had that much [money] on the place" (303)? These glimpses, and the marked discrepancies that emerge in the accounts preserved by the multiple narrators, provide more than the single Caroline Compson we have permitted to dominate the collaborative imagination of the novel. Certainly in the sections not told by Quentin or Jason she is reasonably not the dungeon herself, and only the urge to consistency has imposed such unity on our actual experience of her.

The Mrs. Compson revealed in section two, lying "back in her chair, the camphor handkerchief to her mouth.... [with] the bellowing hammering away like no place for it in silence" (173) is a woman under siege. She is, as she has said repeatedly, "the one who has to bear it" (272). The others can and do go away. Without rhyme or reason, Mrs. Compson remains, incarnated variously as whiner, witch, jailer – scapegoat for nearly all that is wrong with the family Compson. She is the only female Compson remaining in the final section of the 1929 work: she endures creatively, somehow "exhum[ing] from somewhere a sort of fortitude, strength" (299). She waits at the end of the Easter section, guilty of everything save raising Christ from the dead, asking us the question that has assailed her in all of her incarnations: why has God let a lady be treated this way?[35]

April 25, 1910 [Wedding Day]

> *"Well what about it I'm not going to play cards with* [him]" (123)

Though much melancholy ink has been devoted to the multiple Quentins in Faulkner's canon, critics have taken for granted that

Caddy remains the *same.* In following her progress from the top of the tree to beyond the social and textual borders of the Compson domain, we have constructed a Caddy that conforms to the image and logic of character announced and shaped by her creator: "Too beautiful to be reduced to telling."[36] The implications for such beauty and such silence are ominous, and in many ways, Caddy's textual muteness in the 1929 version, and her destiny as a glossy photo in the Appendix, have paradoxically made it easier to believe in the attributes of defiance, courage, and passion that Faulkner claimed for her. But there is a price for female courage and survival, and the woman in the photo has paid it. The Appendix serves up a cautionary apotheosis, a poignant summation fulfilling all our expectations for little girls who climb trees and are braver than their brothers: *"Caddy doesn't want to be saved hasn't anything anymore worth being saved for nothing worth being lost that she can lose"* (342).[37] But there is more to Caddy than loss, or rather, there are more Caddys lost than we have begun to do justice to. Sundquist, in the wake of so many critical suitors, has wryly noted that "There is probably no major character in literature about whom we know so little in proportion to the amount of attention she receives."[38] I would like to extend his claim. Only people's careless ways of using their eyes, as Kate Rainey puts it, has produced a coherent figure with muddy drawers. The Caddy who disappeared from the *The Sound and the Fury* in 1929, presumably finally, once and for all, until she disappeared again in 1946 in that chromium-trimmed sports car into Nazi country – or at least did, before the Appendix disappeared too in 1984 – is *made* unified, that is, becomes Caddy at the expense of all her richer possibilities and troubling inconsistencies.

Even sympathetic readings which want to rescue her from the idea that she is merely an embodiment of natural evil, the source of ruin, force unity on her at every opportunity, and end by seeing her only as Caddy, the victim, one *ruined by* the evil that patriarchy fosters. The Caddy who climbed the tree has been lost to Benjy since "Twilight" and held captive in the prevailing and monolithic readings of the book.[39] Attempts to ransom her from that ostensibly neutral territory of fiction have been undertaken by feminist critics. Minrose Gwin, for instance, has struggled to hear Caddy's voice, but found her silenced in a creative world where oppression is predominantly naturalized.[40] F. D. Faber's unwitting diagnosis of Caddy's "crucial" role clarifies the dilemma for like-minded readers who have maintained they hear the silence: "for Caddy, in the deepest psychological sense, is *in* the men."[41] To insist that she transcends the need for a voice, or that somehow she would have been diminished if granted a voice, is to collaborate with the notorious old stratagem,[42] not in the least mitigated because it is deployed in fiction or poetry: if you are female, the knowledge that urns make great art is a fraught proposition.

Ironically, the Caddy who leaves no message of her own, who has no voice of her own, still manages to signify. She leaves her "mark" though she is reduced to the sounds she precipitates and the signature on her check ritually burned. We do not know how she signs her name, but we recognize her in Benjy's hammering bellow, in Quentin's deafening, misogynistic rant, and in the endorsement on the checks that her daughter may not view and that her mother destroys. We never have the chance to see her purely through the eyes of the two most crucial female affiliations. Represented entirely through male memory, Caddy as a mother is given textual status primarily in Jason's account. But Jason's world dramatizes the extreme diminishment and dependency of women in male economies: "I make it a rule never to keep a scrap of paper bearing a woman's hand, and I never write them at all" (193). As a result of Jason's policy, we have drawn only provisional inferences about how Caddy has reacted to the conditions of banishment, or how she has dealt with it, though clearly separation and rupture are crucial to each of the stories *and* how they are told. Caddy, more perhaps than any other fictive creation anywhere in literature, most purely corresponds to William Gass's insight about fictional character in *Fiction and the Figures of Life*: "A character, first of all, is the noise of *his* name, and all the sounds and rhythms that proceed from *him*" (49; emphasis mine). She is ultimately, even exclusively, the noise of her name: the sound of male anguish each time we meet her, whether she is coming or going, but most especially when she is gone.

Caddy's dominant shape emerges from the "June 2, 1910"

narrative. Suspended in the "liquid putrefaction" of femaleness, Caddy batters at Quentin's memory not as Benjy's comforter, but most immediately in the activities that force Quentin to confront his own virginity, a state valued only in women. Images of Caddy as bride, and the memories of sexual encounters leading up to the wedding invitation Quentin resists opening, seep and eddy through his recollections of his father's nihilistic philosophy. In Quentin's dissolving world, she is nearly always fluid: the Caddy who bravely looked in the window at Damuddy's funeral has already played in the branch. Quentin's search for dissolution in the Charles River foregrounds the watery presence of Caddy, who, as sister, is all mixed up in rain and honeysuckle and mud; appropriately, he recalls her for the last time in his memory of the swing amid the liquefied Compson cedars, where she is metonymically invoked by the reek of perfume with its "vivid dead smell" (176).

Quentin's June suicide protects him from presenting any version of Caddy as mother. In one of the touchstones of his narrative, he remembers her purely as his sister and he recalls a Caddy who is distinctly masculine, never "queen or a fairy." In his obsessed reverie, he recalls Caddy's desire to whip the two dungeonbound characters featured in an illustration in a storybook. Caddy's briefly articulated and more general reaction to the drawing is syntactically subsumed by Quentin's response: he substitutes his parents for the images in the illustration and dreams of disciplining them as Caddy had imagined whipping the vitiated storybook figures languishing in the dark. Though the pages are unaccountably ripped from the book, he is nonetheless obsessed by the picture and darkly gropes for a metaphor to capture his mother, an image that will both contain him and literally as well as figuratively embody his sense of imprisonment. The irresistible transformation of the two figures into his own mother and father leads him to the powerful image of mother as dungeon, a metamorphosis fecundatively Freudian.[43] Rising up as Faulkner's quintessential devouring womb, Mrs. Compson is whipped by Caddy who acts the role of Quentin's accomplice and surrogate, the eroticized and avenging daughter. Whipping the adults for Caddy is not explicitly linked in her mind to her parents: that connection is Quentin's.

But by grafting Quentin's fantasy onto Caddy's desire, critics have generated a daughter who despises her mother and a mother who has become shorthand for such hostility. That Quentin's masculine imagination is host to this female-to-female violence is de-emphasized whereas the worst possibilities of female affiliation are writ large.

Though Quentin's section offers both different and mitigating evidence to remedy this construction of "matrophobia"[44] and a far less assertive Caddy than most commentators have depicted, Quentin's claims that the attic trunks brought down for the husband-seeking safari to French Lick sound like coffins have supported and shaped our attitudes about mother and daughter. As a result, most critics have assumed that Caddy has been utterly coerced into the marriage. But the text itself does not promote that reading; we are not told what and when Mrs. Compson knows of Caddy's condition, or what Mr. Compson is certain of, if anything. The "*voice weeping steadily and softly beyond the twilit door*" (95) as the trunks are prepared for travel is probably Caddy's, but it is impossible to say whether the tears are for the inevitable marriage, the lost Dalton Ames, or the pregnancy itself. We cannot know, though we have been inclined to believe with Quentin, even in his psychosis, that she cries because Mrs. Compson is forcing her to submit to propriety, to find a husband. This belief has encouraged the view of a Mrs. Compson prepared, even eager, to sacrifice her daughter to convention, but such a reading necessarily entails a Caddy whose defiant and passionate insistence on her own sexual desire has evaporated: "*I dont know too many*" (115). She is now willing to surrender her entire identity to oblige the social hypocrisy of her mother and perhaps of her father. The text does suggest that both parents know Caddy has been sexually active, and that there is bound to be gossip. Mr. Compson proposes French Lick as a solution to Caddy's romance with Dalton: "she will forget him then all the talk will die away"; only then does Mrs. Compson speculate that perhaps she "could find a husband for" Caddy (102). At her worst, Mrs. Compson is full of reproach, acting out the rituals of maternal martyrdom. But certainly in 1910, in Mississippi or anywhere else, she was not atypical: many mothers would have reached for the camphor when faced with a pregnant and unmarried daughter. Would we approve of Mrs. Compson more if she had been indifferent to or blithely accepting of Caddy's sexuality? What *do* readers want mothers to do? Mrs. Compson is caught in the double bind of the maternal which Rich describes: "The institution of motherhood finds all mothers more or less guilty of having failed their children."[45] Since the patriarchy has religiously and relentlessly instructed mothers (and their critics) on the role virginity plays in the marketing of daughters (Mr. Compson's cynical comments to his son about purity notwithstanding), Mrs. Compson believes that "people cannot flout God's laws with impunity" (199). She has been indoctrinated in this "truth" from the same sources that have taught Dilsey her lessons. And if Caroline Compson enforces these laws, she does so as an agent of patriarchy: the law of the fathers "protect[s] women from one another from themselves our women ... *they dont acquire knowledge of people we are for that*" (96). Caroline Compson feels right in denying her daughter access to her own child because somewhere she has been instructed that she "owe[s] that to [Mr. Compson's] memory" (220), since "there is no halfway ground ... a woman is either a lady or not" (103).

One-dimensional views of Mrs. Compson see only this coercive and sanctimonious side of her character and tend to dismiss the possibility that she is trapped in her roles too. These readings exclude the possibility that she experiences pain over her own helplessness and the rigidity of the culture that imprisons her in her training. Women's suffering is not *the* subject of *The Sound and the Fury,* but the text does offer readers at least a glimpse of the patriarchy's power to enforce the lessons Mrs. Compson has internalized. Mrs. Compson exposes the role playing mandated by the Compson males when she reveals a telling motive for her frequent "sicknesses," one not much considered by critics who have constructed the dominant portrait of mother as hypochondriac: she reports to Herbert that Quentin and Mr. Compson "both feel a little insulted when I am strong enough to come down to the table" (95). As a bedridden complaining mother, enormously circumscribed by sex, culture, and class, she can meet the needs of an alcoholic husband and a melancholy son while participating in the household dramas her illnesses make possible. Her frequent illnesses draft her husband and sons into gallant, if long-suffering attendants, and because of the belief in female frailty, she can exercise her claims on their attention legitimately. In a world that negates female presence, a mother can become the cynosure of the household through her fragile health: "Is Mother very sick." Caddy asks. "No." Father replies. The blurred connection between illness and female priority is reinforced when we recall that Caddy has only recently made sense of the funeral activities by claiming that her mother and "Damuddy are both sick" (74). Soon Caddy herself will be transformed, and her own desire will be punished by the grammar of the culture, which articulates female desire in metaphors of illness: *"I could see it through them grinning at me through their faces it's gone now and I'm sick"* (112). Marriage and illness are integrally linked in the domestic world of *The Sound and the Fury.*

Allowing for a Mrs. Compson who is pressured to live out the role of mother and invalid makes it possible to imagine and to *believe* that on the eve of packing for French Lick *both* female faces are tearful behind the door. We can and must acknowledge the mutuality of the grief shared behind the door, behind all the doors, since, as Faulkner put it in a short story of this period, "Life in all places is terrible for women."[46] Conscripted entirely by the "proper" choices available to them – as mother and as daughter – what happens behind the door becomes a story of female relationship rivaling the mother/son, sister/brother stories that have dominated our sense of the work. Readers ignore this other story at cost: *"A face reproachful tearful an odor of camphor and of tears a voice weeping steadily and softly beyond the twilit door"* (95). Deeply embedded in this scene resides a painful mutuality. Neither Quentin nor Faulkner can isolate in any clean flame the recursive implications of the sexual and historical trap confronted by this mother and this daughter who will soon become a mother herself. Mutuality is engrained in the mother-daughter plot, but if the plot is never confronted we cannot break the taboo that Rich claims surrounds women's lives and keeps women from one another, prohibits the acknowledgment of female worthiness as birthright.

By neglecting the mother-daughter plot, the dominant culture usurps female energy and focuses attention on the male kinship plots it elects to privilege.[47]

The text is silent on all aspects of Caddy's courtship with Herbert in French Lick, though readers are told that Caddy has talked about Quentin a great deal (or at least that Herbert reports such conversations as a way of perhaps disarming the sullen and resistant brother-in-law). The text does not reveal how Mrs. Compson has conducted herself to bring about the "solution" of Herbert, but when he visits the family, he has clearly succumbed to the effects of mother-daughter collaboration. Mrs. Compson strains to present a unified family front to her daughter's suitor. And although her flirtatious manner with Herbert has been roundly held against her – more evidence of her vanity and narcissism – she seems compelled to try to please. Herbert translates into a car for her daughter, a job for her son, and if she in fact does know about the pregnancy, Herbert equals a father for her grandchild, a way out of pending disgrace were Caddy to remain single and pregnant. Caddy has postponed seeing a doctor to forestall discovery, and she is not so far along that her body betrays her "ruined" condition; she may well count on her mother's eagerness to have her married to mask the specifics of the pregnancy. Or, through what Mr. Compson calls women's "*practical fertility of suspicion,*" Mrs. Compson may have figured it out. There remains also the possibility that Caddy may have enlisted Mrs. Compson in the French Lick marriage project without telling her everything. Mrs. Compson may know everything, as Joan Williams has persuasively argued, if Caddy has confided in her, counting on her support in this crisis. If so, then Caddy's unhappiness and tears need not be rooted in her mother's response, or even in the doom of respectable marriage; mother and daughter may well have charted together as coconspirators. The tears may be prompted by the biology of her condition, triggered by a recognition of the diminished freedom she now faces as the future Mrs. Head. They may even be for the little girl from "Twilight" who failed to "run away and never come back" (19) and must now go instead to South Bend by way of French Lick – all the way to Indiana.

Caddy may be stuck, tearful, trapped, and desperate, but she does not appear to feel doomed. As a young woman, she has repeatedly violated the taboos of the patriarchy. Voicing her own desires with Dalton and Herbert and Charlie and all the "too many," she has risked taking herself to market.[48] Bowed, Caddy practically and sanely balks at Quentin's scruples over Herbert's "disgrace" at Harvard. She offers virtually the only comic relief in the June 2, 1910, narration when she reacts to Quentin's shocked disclosure that Herbert has been dropped by his club for cheating: "*Well what about it I'm not going to play cards with* [him]" (123). Her bluntness reminds us that Herbert is the way to satisfy the edict, agreement, understanding, or compromise: She must marry quickly if she is pregnant, must in any case marry someone eventually.

I believe our reactions to Caddy's "capitulation," her matter-of-fact attitude about Herbert Head for husband, have a great deal to do with how we read her claim to have "*died last year*" (123). In the process of becoming unvirgin she mimics the passion of romance: she tells Quentin "I would die for [Ames] Ive already died for him I die for him over and over again every time this goes" (151). But once pregnant, caught in the machinery of propriety, Caddy will be expected to play out the role of the good daughter, as well as fulfill that of the proper wife. She enlists Quentin, or tries to. With her father drinking himself to death, and Benjy vulnerable to institutionalization, she exhorts Quentin to tend to things, to assume the role of caretaker. She finds no room in the script for tears: "*I cant cry I cant even cry one minute*" (124). As literary convention has constructed it, sexual passion, so like dying in its annihilation of self, has been translated into social dying: "*now I know I'm dead I tell you*" (124). Her own desires are irrelevant – even to her. The variety of assignments prescribed for her converge in the imminent wedding and she relinquishes her role as dutiful daughter for her new role as dutiful bride. She intends to salvage the family honor which she has been trained to put ahead of personal identity: "*What else can I think about what else have I thought about. . . . I cant even cry I died last year I told you I had but I didn't know then what I meant I didn't know what I was saying*" (123). No longer Benjy's Caddy, she exits through the mirror, a trace of dead perfume. Indiana offers neither comfort nor escape. Her illicit pregnancy has canceled her value in the system of exchange; as "a fallen woman" she can no longer operate as valuable currency in the patriarchal economy. To the extent that she can circulate in the interest of male pleasure – feminine or maternal, she is desired; in sabotaging these two assigned identities, Caddy finds herself sanctioned and she in effect does *die.* Exiled from Benjy's twilight, she will now remove from Eden, and cease to incarnate yet another version of her permutating self. Textually she becomes a ghost hovering by gravesites, negotiating for glimpses of and information about her daughter; her utter loss of agency and identity dramatizes fully how much motherhood is the province of the masculine.

The Caddy who exists under the regime of Jason must resort to futilely pleading with him for compassion, begging him to make sure that Quentin "has things like other girls." The familiar Jason, speaking with the authority of fathers, replies: "Sure. . . . As long as you behave and do like I tell you" (210). Not only has the defiant Caddy ceased to be, she is barely a tic from her indomitable girlhood. We cannot even see the vestige of her former self, though Jason believes he can feel it.

> [W]hen she'd get mad and couldn't do anything about it her upper lip would begin to jump. Everytime it jumped it would leave a little more of her teeth showing, and all the time she'd be as still as a post, not a muscle moving except for her lip jerking higher and higher up her teeth. But she didn't say anything. (208)

Under what revision of his character would the Caddy of section three imagine that Jason would honor any commitment, respond to any appeal to family or female need? Still, this Caddy attempts to negotiate with Jason for the chance to see her child. Her only retaliation takes the form of a small resistance to the economic machinery; in Irigarayan vocabulary, she "jams" the system of the fathers by mailing her support check later than Jason believes is appropriate. As the law reduced to its pettiest form, an exasperated Jason wonders, "How long would a man that thought the first of the month came on the sixth last in business" (190). That he is an exploiter of his sister and mother and a brutalizer of his niece makes him the perfect site and occasion to examine the heart of oppression wherein social exploitation is integral to the sexual exploitation of women.[49]

The Caddy presented by Jason is unfamiliar. No longer the bold child or the brazen adolescent, she is least like the woman who believed she "can make [Dalton] believe anytime" (163). Even the Caddy who was able to challenge and taunt Jason has disappeared; this Caddy is undone by all his crass attempts at retribution. It is hard to see the Caddy of the branch or the Caddy who has survived Dalton, or even the Caddy who has finessed a marriage to an eligible bachelor in this slinking and defeated Caddy. Even the practical Caddy who "has to marry someone" has ceased to exist when she stammers and pleads with Jason to let her see her daughter. Either the breakup with Herbert has so altered her that she bears no resemblance to her former selves or she has been utterly transformed by the loss of her child and banishment from the household. Implicit in this Caddy's defeat is a maternal echo and legacy; she poses a version of the very question Mrs. Compson asked – why *has* God let a woman be treated this way?

QUENTIN Monday April 9, 1928 [Truant Days]

> "Whether or not she was in school today
> is past," I says. "If you've got to worry
> about it, worry about next Monday." (260)

Caddy's daughter is a reminder to Jason of his governing doctrine: "Once a bitch always a bitch" (180). As one of the most quoted lines in all of Faulkner, Jason's doctrine further reminds us of the core of misogyny running through the dominant culture, which makes the expressions of this sentiment not taboo, but funny and familiar: women are essentially "the same," fused, undifferentiated, and indistinguishable one from the other in the male imaginary.[50] At best, Caddy's daughter, like Caddy herself, Mrs. Compson, and even Damuddy, have ontological status in the culture Faulkner depicts for their single recognized and sanctioned function – as mothers.[51] And since maternal identity achieves value only as it bears, literally and figuratively, on the masculine, Quentin's role as Caddy's daughter has been ancillary to the various discussions of mothering in the work.[52] Critics eager to comment on Caddy's maternal and nurturing role with Benjy have been less inclined to focus on the particulars of her maternal relationship with Quentin. When Caddy's daughter is discussed, she becomes the occasion to stress the emotional poverty in the 1928 Jason-dominated household. In such readings, Jason and his cruel exploitation are the real subject; Caddy, Mrs. Compson, and Quentin are merely the interchangeable objects of great masculine villainy. Consideration of the mother-daughter plot gives way to an emphasis on brother-sister, uncle-niece, and son-mother connections. Each axis includes a female, but male experience *naturally* assumes priority. Speaking in the idiom of patriarchy, Dalton Ames, who never had a sister, asserts the "knowledge" that is his birthright. He lucidly and confidently reminds Quentin, and so all of us, about the systemic reduction integral to the exercise of patriarchal privilege: "no but theyre all bitches" (160).

Quentin's story, emerging primarily from Jason's account, is in many ways the least contested narrative in the Compson family.[53] Attracting little sustained critical attention, Quentin has no immediate male line – no father, no brother, no son – to make her "important."[54] Constructed from the economically obsessed narrative offered by Jason, Quentin represents, in Jason's mind, his economic grievances. Hostage to the Compson household, sent there by never-disclosed pressures, Quentin is both another tragic little girl and the *same* one. As Faulkner's own perverse rendering of *The Scarlet Letter*, she is the living Q, named for her suicidal uncle, and she offers an apotheosis of the social and economic exploitation of women in the world of *The Sound and the Fury*. As "merchandise," the role assigned to all women in Irigaray's critique of the patriarchal economy,[55] she is the mechanism by which Jason tries to balance the ledger. Driven by his economy of revenge, Jason reveals in his exploitation of Quentin and her mother nearly every device deployed by patriarchy to render women interchangeable and so maintain the "infrastructure" of male exchange.[56] Jason perpetually negotiates and calculates the losses he has suffered at the hands of the world in general, but especially women, and most specifically Caddy.[57] Her daughter, the treachery made flesh, is the "bitch that cost [him] . . . a job" (304). For Jason, Quentin is simply a commodity in the system that he controls: "I never promise a woman anything nor let her know what I'm going to give her. That's the only way to manage them" (193). He extorts money from his gullible mother; he keeps Lorraine in line and out of Jefferson with reminders to think of the forty dollars and count to ten; he sells Caddy the right to glimpse her daughter for one hundred dollars; and he torments Quentin, withholding money and letters from her mother. Quentin has merged so completely with Jason's calculations of financial loss that "Neither of them had had entity or individuality for him for ten years" (306).

Jason's use of Quentin as commodity illustrates Irigaray's critique of the sexual, economic, and cultural exchange enforced by masculine systems. Irigaray identifies it as "*specific exploitation*," by which a woman is rendered "the object of a transaction" and who, through her "use, consumption, and circulation . . . underwrite[s] the organization and the reproduction of the social order."[58] Woman's interchangeability and the intersection of sex and economy create the "grammar" of his cruel discourse:[59]

> [T]hen he thought of the money again, and that he had been outwitted by a woman, a girl. If he could just believe it was the man who had robbed him. But to have been robbed of that which was to have compensated him for the lost job, which he had acquired through so much effort and risk, by the very symbol of the lost job itself, and worst of all, by a bitch of a girl. (307)

Irigaray's examination of the systemic nature of male mastery is at the heart of Jason's lament that "it takes a white man not to have anymore sense than to worry about what a little slut of a girl does" (243). The complicit nature of "tragic fiction" and the role tragic fiction plays in the maintenance of the masculine imaginary can be glimpsed in a telling example from the criticism about Quentin. One such master engaged in the production of "truth," Cleanth Brooks, offers a virulent assessment of Quentin:

> The disintegration that took place in the Compson family after Jason became its head is revealed most clearly and terribly in the character of Candace's daughter, Quentin. *The child is nearly every thing that Jason bitterly accuses her of being:* she is a cheap little wanton, offering herself to almost any man who puts in an appearance, and

> in her wantonness she resembles her mother. But the daughter lacks certain virtues that her mother possessed: graciousness, pity, and disinterested love. . . .
>
> She is cheap and thoughtless, and she has absorbed from her uncle something of his cruelty.[60]

Brooks goes on to contextualize the deforming processes affecting Quentin IV's character; he acknowledges fully how frustrated and unhappy she is, warped in much the same way he believes Joe Christmas was by Doc Hines's brutality. To Brooks, Faulkner's "unsentimental" treatment of Quentin keeps her from being merely a victim, and renders her instead "his bitterest judgment" on Jason. Brooks's phrasing, so particularly evocative of Mrs. Compson's own, oddly inflects his authority. It is noteworthy in the realm of sexual/textual politics that Brooks's discussion of Quentin hinges on confidence in, if not quite solidarity with, Jason as a reliable reporter of his niece's activities. By the time Brooks and Jason have had their say, male tragedy asserts its hold on all experience and female sexuality is shown clearly to be the cause of male misery. All in all, this is far too instructive an example of the patriarchal agendas potentially served by both *The Sound and the Fury* and its canonical guards. Indignant and righteous, Brooks's assessment of Quentin and his inclination to validate Jason's narrative should make even the staunchest believer in "objective" scholarship think twice. Between a slut and a monster, Brooks apparently will take the monster.

I would like to turn now to the repressed dimensions of Quentin's character, and show that much like Mrs. Compson and Caddy, she is not unifiable. Far less stable and verifiable than Jason and Brooks would have readers believe, Quentin has been assembled to support the social order's "fiction" of sexuality. By and large, Quentin derives her textual presence from *not being* – she is not in school and she is not in her room. Luster reports that she regularly slips out, and that Mrs. Compson routinely locks Quentin's door. But nowhere in the text is it clear that Mrs. Compson's lock and key policy is caused by a pattern of behavior, or even an incident. If it's "in the blood," then Mrs. Compson seems determined to manage her granddaughter's chastity and whereabouts for the sake of her husband's memory, and for her son's reputation.

Readers should keep in mind that Luster tells his tale to the man in the red tie and his word has lent authority to readings of Quentin as sexually transgressive: "They comes every night" (50). But the "shiny" condom container precipitating the conversation is not described further (50).[61] It is important to remember that Luster is not above lies and distortions, and that he is eager to ingratiate himself with the potential golf ball buyer. Asking Luster to name the visitor from the previous evening, the buyer jokes about "the track" of rubber left by this particular predator (50). The man in the red tie, in town only briefly, lacks a particular knowledge of Miss Quentin. Yet, he, like Jason and Brooks, finds against Quentin. We are encouraged to share the view of her as sexualized, "a slut," and the words and assumptions of Jason, Luster, and the red-tie man all are instantly rendered credible because – well, we know a bitch when we see one – and even if we don't *actually* see one. Miss Quentin's circulation guarantees protection to the social order that recognizes male subjectivity exclusively. Jason speaks, however colloquially, the same laws of the fathers, when he suspects that Quentin, his "object," has acted on her own desire:[62] "Do you think I can afford to have her running about the streets with every drummer that comes to town, I says, and them telling the new ones up and down the road where to pick up a hot one when they made Jefferson" (230). Though Miss Quentin challenges Jason's law and dares "anybody to know everything," she does not admit to any specific sexual encounter. The text does not offer resolution. Her defiance could be rooted in a variety of resistances; her whereabouts while truant are revealed only on this one day. Challenging Jason's role as provider, she prefers to tear off her dress rather than wear something he paid for (188), and though she audaciously claims to prefer life in hell over life with Jason (180), elsewhere she seems less the brazen resister of his law than the desperately lost child: "Dilsey, I want my mother" (185).

Her bravado fluctuates not just in section three of the novel but in each of her appearances in the work. Like the Caddys who are brave and defiant, Quentin intermittently resembles her mother in resistance to authority, and there are correspondences to the daunted Caddy as well. Though his focus is not on the parallels in the mother-daughter plot, Bleikasten has perceptively observed that Jason's obsession with Quentin's sexuality is both parallel to and a near parody of her namesake's obsession with her mother.[63] Even Quentin's furtive presence in the text recalls Caddy. Quentin, like the Caddys, is often not there, and when she is, she is available only through the filter of male narrative. Missing most of the time, she counters her erasure in the masculine imaginary by creating a self, "her face all gummed up with paint" (187); like her mother and her mother's mother, she complies with "this masquerade of femininity" which is "imposed upon women by male systems of representation."[64] Her boldness is offset by other examples of behavior where she seems more a pleading cipher – pleading for money, for the right to read her mother's letter (214), for an explanation of Jason's unprovoked cruelty. She must even plead for more coffee.

Quentin's presence has been pieced together out of some brief but charged scenes that punctuate her absences. She has given Luster a quarter in section one (72); in section three her principal has called and she, behind her closed door, may or may not be reading books that she may or may not own. Though she does threaten to run away in section one, she exhibits little of the desperation so marking her responses in Jason's narrative. And unless Brooks turns out to be the man Jason claims had his car all afternoon and knows things we don't know, Brooks speaks with more authority than he should "about such wickedness." Suspicion and certitude about Quentin's "wanton activity" impose far sharper critical definition on her than the text actually supplies.

Occupying the room next to the pear tree, apparently Caddy's room, she, like the room, is physically bereft. Quentin's face, according to Jason, looks as if she had "polished it with a gun rag" (184), and he likens her nose to a "porcelain insulator" (257). When she makes her escape, Faulkner describes the room as "not anybody's room, and the faint scent of cheap cosmetics and the few feminine objects and the other evidences of crude and hopeless efforts to feminize it but added to its anonymity, giving it that dead and stereotyped transience of rooms in assignation houses" (282). Even the "forlorn scent of blossoms" from the pear tree outside the room fails to attach itself to Quentin, and so sharpens the contrast with her mother, redolently connected to trees, to perfume, to honeysuckle.

But Caddy's poor abandoned daughter and Jason's desperate and bewildered captive challenges the ugly blankness and deprivation of Jason's controlling and limiting perspective. She is more than the single, empty, and sexualized female he "imagines." Readings like Brooks's which tend to focus on her sexuality and/or the extreme emptiness of her world in the tragic 1928 Compson household, do not adequately account for the other dimensions of Quentin latent in the text. If we resist Jason's instruction – that we've "got to learn *one* thing, and that is that when I tell you to do something, you've got it to do" (215; emphasis mine) – we can produce a reading of Quentin that allows her to be more than a reduced and pathetic figure.

Seeing her only as slut, Jason can only misread her. When her eyes "turned kind of funny" (188), he assumes she is about to cry. When he accuses her of slipping around, she reminds him that what she does she does openly. Jason's bathetic pursuit of her is not only in broad daylight, but in the crucial hours of stock market trading. Later, as he attempts to bait and torment her, he describes her eyes as "cornered" (259), and he believes he has routed her from his table; we recall that Caddy has also been described as having "eyes like cornered rats" (149).[65] Ultimately, whatever misery she has experienced, however profound her lament that her life is unbearable, Quentin just as seriously demonstrates her own nascent capacity to "jam" systems.[66] As she directs her comments to her grandmother, she speaks the unspeakable. She asks for an accounting for Jason's cruelty, and nearly violates the prohibition on her mother's name: "If he doesn't want me here, why wont he let me go back to – " (259). Beyond these disruptions, she refuses finally to be "solid," and in the first version of her escape, she embodies all the qualities of disruptive and fluid excess: "*We watched the tree shaking. The shaking went down the tree, then it came out and we watched it go away across the grass*" (74). In her earlier fight with Jason all the triumph of fluid has been presaged: "*She picked up her glass of water and swung her arm back, looking at Jason. Dilsey caught her arm. They fought. The glass broke on the table, and the water ran into the table. Quentin was running''* (71). It is worth remembering that Jason, a rabid patriarch and curator of the values of the solid economy, admits that "just to look at water makes [him] sick" (233). He shares this horror of fluids with his brother Quentin who twice in Benjy's section "wish[es] it wouldn't rain" (66).

That Quentin can finally leave Jefferson without regret may in part be owing to Caddy's maternal, albeit distant and meager support. Jason reveals that Caddy has come to town "once or twice a year sometimes" (211), and Quentin appears at last to read her mother's letters: her grandmother will "let [her] see [them]" (212). Quentin even opens the possibility of extra-forbidden contact when she insists she knows a particular letter will contain money: "She promised she would" (213). Quentin is about to emancipate herself with indirect help from her mother, to make good on the threat to leave, to endure no longer the horrible "truth" about life with the Compson men: *"How can anybody live in a house like this"* (69). Jason, disabled by the relentless economic lens, is about to be vanquished: "It made me so mad for a minute it kind of blinded me" (188). Quentin accomplishes exactly what feminine style, in its *"disruptive excess,"* must do: "Its 'style' resists and explodes every firmly established form, figure, idea or concept."[67] As Jason fantasizes apprehending Quentin and the man she is with, Faulkner's language presents Jason as literally "disturbed, driven to distraction."[68] The ideal male authority is made unstable:

> That they should not be there, that the whole result should not hinge on whether he saw them first or they saw him first, would be opposed to *all nature and contrary to the whole rhythm of events.* And more than that: he must see them first, get the money back, then what they did would be of no importance to him, while otherwise the whole world would know that he, Jason Compson, had been robbed by Quentin, his niece, a bitch. (308–9, emphasis mine)

The Appendix elaborates recursively Jason's anguish over the robbery. The Quentin conjured for this 1946 version is granted textual space but is not developed materially in it. Instead, Quentin's story is absorbed by Jason's and we learn his history of extortion and his impotent dreams of revenge in detail. Her method of escape is no longer the tree outside her window, but a rainpipe. According to the voice of the Appendix, Quentin will never marry. Given Faulkner's own marital history, one pauses at the irony he employed in "dooming" Quentin this particular way (346). A soothsayer, Faulkner does not see a Mercedes or a ranking Nazi official in Quentin's future.

Having done what Irigaray claims is strictly forbidden to women,[69] Quentin has acted in her own interest. She has finally, but not fatally, vanished. Irigaray specifically explores the difficulty, if not the impossibility, of even imagining "some other mode of exchange(s) that might not obey the same logic. Yet . . . [this would be] the condition for the emergence of something of woman's language and woman's pleasure. . . . [and] it would have to happen 'elsewhere.' "[70] The power of the phallocracy is perhaps most deeply felt in its capacity to prevent escape. But Irigaray posits a realm "elsewhere"[71] that challenges the masculine imaginary and all it constructs for women and all it forbids them of their own pleasure and identity. In this realm, the mother-daughter plot *would be* central. I like to think that along this underground frailroad[72] there are many signs enabling women who are bound for liberation from the male gaze, from captivity in masculine narrative, and masculine imagination. In disappearing from the Compson world into futures unimaginable, Caddy and her daughter accomplish the escapes crucial to resistance. If mother and daughter are ever to "relearn" affiliation and experience it as life giving, then they must not choose mourning and paralysis. These are the traps set for women in "the Father's drama."[73] Caddy and Quentin reject the versions of mothering offered by Mrs. Compson. In their resistance can be found the alternatives to masculine imaginary. If they are truly en route to "elsewheres" then I like to think that they are reading and leaving signs for other women who will work in the collaborative enterprise of creating the feminine imaginary. Perhaps one such marker could be located just outside of Jefferson. Caddy passed it on her trips back from and to the wherever; and clearly Quentin, headed in the same direction as her mother, passed it too as she traveled beyond the limits of Jefferson. Both Caddy and her daughter have resisted the laws of the fathers and pursue the ek-static.[74] There is no longer a need to ask the question that so bedeviled Mrs. Compson about why God lets ladies be treated *this way*. Reading and writing in order to create a feminine imaginary[75] requires only that we ask ourselves which way to the exteriority. With Caddy and Quentin as our guides, we need only look at the secret already tactilely present in the text: "Keep your on Mottson" (311).

DILSEY [An (Other) Day]

"Den you do de same thing dis Sunday." (318)

In the final section of *The Sound and the Fury*, both the Compson daughters have taken their leave. Miss Quentin has left behind an unspecified and soiled undergarment, surely in homage to her forebear who used the tree outside the window first. A wisp of stocking dangles from the drawer. Still pondering why God has permitted her to be treated this way, Mrs. Compson, for the first and only time, manages to say "mother" in reference to Caddy (299). Beyond this single reference, Caddy exists only as the sound that sets Benjy to wailing: "Here, caddie. Bring the bag" (315).

Since Irigaray's philosophy has inspired my analysis, I would like to take this occasion to practice her theory – to resist: "It is essential for women among themselves to invent new modes of organization, new forms of struggle, new challenges." As long as women allow themselves to be "mastered," caught in "the trap of power, in the game of authority . . . they have nothing more to say or do *as women*."[76] If I were after mastery and were to comply with the conventions of the academy, I would be compelled to take up Dilsey and her daughter in this "penultimate" section. But this section is no more Dilsey's than *The Sound and the Fury* is Caddy's. *The Sound and the Fury* operates in an economy where narrative control is the sine qua non for consideration, and though this Easter Sunday section has been claimed for Dilsey, it has been appropriated by the male voice of Rev. Shegog. Dilsey may endure transcendentally in the economy sanctioned by the fathers, but she is still an unvoiced black woman, sitting in a pew, listening to their voices. Her section even closes with male sounds as Jason and Benjy make cacophonous chorus in the square.

In place of the traditional focus for this April 8, 1928, section, I should like to claim this space for a muster of all the women who are denied voice in this text, who have had status only as they are circulated in the masculine imaginary. Remember, this is a muster, "not a segregation" (225).

Quentin Maclachan's mother	Mrs. Bland
Damuddy	Gerald's women
Agnes	the bakery woman
Mabel	Little Sister
Becky	the woman with a shawl
Natalie	Lorraine
Little Sister Death	Dilsey
Dalton Ames's mother	Frony
Miss Laura	the "sistuhns" at Dilsey's church
Miss Holmes	Mary the mother of Jesus
Miss Daingerfield	Myrtle

Leda

APPENDIX/GENEALOGY [Melissa Meek's Day Off][77]

"One day in 1943, after a week of a distraction bordering on disintegration almost" (337)

Melissa Meek. Jefferson County librarian who at approximately forty-eight years of age, in 1943 becomes so obsessed with her former classmate's photo she evidences all the symptoms of disintegration. Unmarried, her irregular, distracted, oddly passionate conduct suggests to the "wives of the bankers and doctors and lawyers" (former classmates as well) "abnormality," makes them believe she is on the "verge of illness" or even derangement. She acts against every rule of proper mouse colored librarianship and "strides" to Jason's store, "that gloomy cavern which only men ever entered" (338). Caddy of course has been there before and the bond between Melissa and Caddy makes it right that both would violate this male sanctuary. Caddy went there to plead for the right to see her daughter; Melissa has come to honor a bond of friendship that has endured for thirty-odd separating years. Melissa "strides" into the cavern past the men who assemble in Jason's domain with its near-parodic resemblance to Plato's cave. She is shocked at her own resources, galvanized into action by her awareness of Caddy's glossy recapture in the labyrinthine world of the masculine and its gaze. Melissa, who knows that Caddy "must be saved," shares neither the narrator's nor the brothers' nor the critics' sense of Caddy as "damned." Abandoning her rule of silence with Jason, in force since Caddy's heir made her escape down that metamorphosed pear tree, she calls him by name, and insists he acknowledge Caddy's face – and so her peril.

Her request that he "see" Caddy and her danger prompts Jason only to scorn. By dismissing her claims, by erasing Caddy and the explicit nature of Melissa's investment in Caddy's danger, Jason instinctively refuses to endorse female affiliation. Since women are only objects for circulation, he actively seeks to keep women separate and alienated one from another. Melissa's explanation illuminates her awareness of the strategies. When Caddy is imperiled, she can exist for Jason; when Caddy is the subject of care – even, or especially, Melissa Meek's – he elects to deny Caddy and Melissa's reality. To *admit* Caddy, to *see* her, would restore Caddy to the realm of female community. Melissa Meek has been temporarily transformed: no longer handmaiden of the library and curator of the words of the fathers housed in the facility, she has become a disrupter, an agent of change, transformed by her desire to intervene and interrogate the fatal forces of the social order. This present tense encounter shows the many shapes of masculine power, and frames the difficulty for women who are heading toward the feminine imaginary: a Nazi staffgeneral is yet another version of Jason.

In Memphis, Melissa reports Jason's behavior to Dilsey and her account makes explicit how the "*position of mastery*"[78] preserves and perpetuates its privilege. But her efforts to get Dilsey to "look" fail as well. She leaves Memphis by bus, surrounded by the teeming population "enroute either to leave or to death." The young women surrounding her are homeless and the world is bleak. On the bus as Melissa weeps over all she has done and felt, she is literally transported by "a shape"; a man lifts her doll-like into a seat next to the window, a forceful demonstration of the dominant culture's power to police its property, acting to put a wayward librarian, forty-eight and unmarried, back in the place where she belongs.

"Properly" repositioned, she is thrown back to reflect on the dreamy nightmare that constitutes her fictional reality in Jefferson. The unmarried librarian, awaiting absorption by the forces of the town, imagines her existence in fictional terms – contained within a text: "at six oclock you could close the covers on it and even the weightless hand of a child could put it back among its unfeatured kindred on the quiet eternal shelves and turn the key upon it for the whole and dreamless night" (342). The account is surreal, complicating seriously the boundaries between fiction and fictional reality. Melissa Meek, for the time being, has been vanquished; patriarchal operations restore her to the library that paradoxically contains and empowers her. She is possessed by both the text and the source of its circulation. In her library dominion, she controls the circulation and the access. But it is a circumscribed exercise of feminine authority, since she is contained in the larger world that contains such libraries. It is also an old story that contains her, since life is over there on the shelf. In her imaginings, Melissa can, at the end of the day, close the volume, *shelve* the texts that tell the single story of masculine desire and despair, valorized one way or another as *our* heart's darling. The culture that excludes female subjectivity does not allow more than *one* story. Ultimately it offers a horrific vision of the idealization of art – it is stilled life. For readers of *The Sound and the Fury,* who look *and* see Melissa Meek, however, neither she nor Caddy has been swept away by dishonor and time. Casting shadows of their own, absolutely on the move, both to Memphis, Germany, and Paris – even if some of us are stalled in Jefferson – Melissa and Caddy present in the Appendix a model of the caring possibilities yet to be realized, clearly in the offing. Melissa's quiet but passionate concern for Caddy in the face of rejection and denial relays a different message about the desirability of ordered places and the idealism of the masculine imaginary where they both reside – one a heart's darling, the other tenuously in the work if at all. Melissa Meek, unmarried librarian, reminds us of the defiant potential to be found in Caddy and Quentin, two other women who did not refuse to look. Like Melissa they offer readers who are equally unafraid of looking some different versions of passion and bravery. More than one, all enduring.

NOTES

1 Clifton Fadiman, "Hardly Worth the Wait," in *Critical Essays on William Faulkner: The Compson Family,* ed. Arthur Kinney (Boston: G.K. Hall, 1982), p. 93.

2 Winfield Townley Scott, "[Review]" in *William Faulkner: The Critical Heritage,* ed. John Bassett (Boston: Routledge & Kegan Paul, 1975), p. 82.

3 Philip Weinstein presented this argument at the 1990 American Literature Association meeting in a talk as yet unpublished entitled "Canon Musings: Why Is *The Sound and the Fury* 'Our Heart's Darling'?" Weinstein argued that there is a cybernetics of pleasure available for the male teacher of literature through the teaching and reteaching of *The Sound and the Fury,* and finds that it valorizes patriarchal classroom practices in a particularly irresistible way. Since the talk did not deal with the relationship of the work to teachers who were not white and male, its canonical status as "heart's darling" seems less secure as more diverse faculty participate in the shaping of modernism. See also Weinstein's *Faulkner's Subject: A Cosmos No One Owns* (New York: Cambridge University Press, 1992).

4 See Polk's introduction to this volume.

5 For examples of this approach, see Douglas Messerli, "The Problem of Time in *The Sound and the Fury:* A Critical Reassessment and Reinterpretation," *Southern Literary Journal* 6.2 (Spring 1974): 37–41; see also Carvel Collins, "The Interior Monologues of *The Sound and the Fury,*" in *English Language Institute Essays 1952,* ed. Alan S. Downer (New York: Columbia University Press, 1954), pp. 53–6.

6 See Eileen Gregory, "Caddy Compson's World," in *The Merrill Studies in The Sound and the Fury,* ed. James B. Meriwether (Columbus, Ohio: Charles E. Merrill, 1970), pp. 89–101. Gregory's notes provide a thorough and thoughtful history and range of summary of the treatment accorded Caddy in the criticism through the sixties (see especially p. 90, note 3). Since the 1970s, Caddy has figured consistently in most studies of *The Sound and the Fury* and I will mention many of them in the course of my analysis. She has enjoyed a sort of critical boom and perhaps has even become the victim of "overproduction." The beautiful one who never had her own narrative was even given her own book when Harold Bloom brought out a volume on Caddy Compson in Chelsea House's Major Literary Characters series. Caddy, with other Major Literary Characters in Bloom's stable like Ahab, Lady Brett, and even Satan, counts in her staff entourage an assistant art

director and a picture researcher. It is worth noting that despite the fact that Caddy has been examined as everything from the female principle to the narrative core, she has not been studied in the context of female affiliations.

7 Eric J. Sundquist, *Faulkner: The House Divided* (Baltimore: Johns Hopkins University Press, 1985), p. 10.

8 Ibid., p. 12.

9 Cheryl Lester, "From Place to Place in *The Sound and the Fury:* The Syntax of Interrogation," *Modern Fiction Studies* 34.2 (1988): 141–56. Cheryl Lester has gracefully characterized the particular critical tendency to identify the sections of *The Sound and the Fury* with their narrators as being so "endemic" that it cannot be "exhaustively describe[d]" (143). Although I find her entirely persuasive and clear-headed in analysis of the failures and dodges produced by chronological and point-of-view readings of the novel, I disagree with the premise she repeats twice in her opening arguments: "the individual sections of *The Sound and the Fury* are not intelligible in themselves" (141).

10 My point here is in the spirit of the delicious paradoxes generated in Gerald Graff's *Literature Against Itself: Literary Ideas in Modern Society* (Chicago: University of Chicago Press, 1979), p. 36. For instance, the chaos introduced and mindlessly restored at the end of *The Sound and the Fury* serves most teachers as an occasion to wax eloquent on the loss of meaningful tradition. Yet, as we talk about the collapse of order, in the work so cunningly contrived to demonstrate disorder, there is a crisis of authenticity. Or as Graff puts it: "Romantic esthetics typifies the more general crisis of modern thought, which pursues a desperate quest for meaning in experience while refusing to accept the validity of any meaning proposed."

See also Sally Woolf and David Minter, "A 'Matchless Time': Faulkner and the Writing of *The Sound and the Fury,*" in *Writing the American Classics,* eds. James Barbour and Tom Quirk (Chapel Hill: University of North Carolina Press, 1990), pp. 156–76. The conclusions Woolf and Minter come to typify the irresistibility of any readings that are not tame and familiar.

11 Luce Irigaray exhorts women not to be fearful of violating the traditions of linearity, to resist the cultural pressures to write, organize, think, and express in the "same" way prescribed and sanctioned by patriarchy. In this spirit I play with Faulknerian dogma and formal structures of the essay, even permitting myself to contradict and reverse myself if such disruptions will create pleasure. See *This Sex Which*

Is Not One, trans. Catherine Porter with Carolyn Burke (Ithaca: Cornell University Press, 1985), p. 203.

12 William Faulkner, *The Sound and the Fury. The Corrected Text with Faulkner's Appendix* (New York: Modern Library, 1992), p. 173. All further references to the text will be from this volume, documented parenthetically.

13 Irigaray, *This Sex*, p. 112.

14 See Luce Irigaray, particularly her essay "And the One Doesn't Stir without the Other," *Signs* 7.1 (1981): 60–7. Though I do not believe we have as yet discovered the grammar necessary to resist the relentless pull of the Same as it operates to systematize experience, unless we engage the text on some other basis than "women as lovely and tragic victim and perpetual object of desire," we will find it hard to break free of the critical tradition – or to imagine new ways of reading this book or changing the world we read in. Since tragedy has almost exclusively been understood in terms of masculine experience, readings of Caddy that shed light on the masculine tragedy but not on "her tragedy" tell us much about how systematically excluded female experience is from ethical examination. (*This Sex*, p. 30)

15 Malcolm Cowley, *The Faulkner-Cowley File: Letters and Memories 1944–1962* (New York: Viking, 1966), p. 90.

16 See Graff, *Literature Against Itself*, on the resistance of systems to challenge from competing authorities and alternative readings (p. 189).

17 Irigaray, *This Sex*, p. 157.

18 Adrienne Rich, *Of Woman Born: Motherhood as Experience and Institution* (New York: Bantam, 1977), p. 226.

19 Ibid., p. 257.

20 Ibid., p. 240.

21 Faulkner's claim that Caddy was "too beautiful and too moving to reduce her to telling what was going on" (Frederick L. Gwynn and Joseph L. Blotner, *Faulkner in the University* [New York: Vintage, 1959], p. 1) is a gallant version of "for her own good." He is surely participating in an old and very unexperimental approach to women's voices. The politics of depriving women of their own voice has been vastly documented as a strategy of patriarchal control in studies like Adrienne Rich's in *On Lies, Secrets, and Silence: Selected Prose 1966–1978* (New York: Norton, 1980), Marilyn Frye's *The Politics of Reality* (New York: Crossing Press, 1984), and *Women's Reality* (New York: HarperCollins, 1991) by Ruth Schaef, and even Tillie Olsen's *Silences* (New York: Dell, 1989). Faulkner approximates the patriarchal strategy that "protects" women from higher earnings, and relieves them

of the burden of deciding about their own biological and reproductive health through a fictional design which relies exclusively on three males and a public authorial voice. He keeps women in the novel where they function as contained subjects. In no way do I wish my argument to be construed as one for parity of women's voices. If Caddy is given no voice of her own, then I prefer to consider the implications of the "voice" she does have.

Though I cannot elaborate my objections here, I would like to note that certain critics of Faulkner mount what can only be seen as complicated arguments for the silencing of women in their defenses of the rightfulness of Caddy's exclusion from voice on grounds other than aesthetic. Stephen Ross, at least entertaining the possibility of implicit misogyny in his *Fiction's Inexhaustible Voice: Speech and Writing in Faulkner* (Athens: University of Georgia Press, 1989), makes an attempt to negotiate this symptom of Faulkner's "ambivalence" toward women, but in concluding he declares the justice in Faulkner's strategy since in terms of the novel "She must remain mute, for she *is* Psyche, bereft, tortured by Venus, and abandoned to silence" (p. 184).

22 Ben Wasson, *Count No 'Count: Flashbacks to Faulkner* (Jackson: University Press of Mississippi, 1983), p. 84. In giving priority to female qua female experience which saturates the text, I hope to get at some alternative readings. Faulkner indirectly authorized such an approach in one of his own metaphors for creation: "like the mother that had four bad children" (David Minter, ed., *The Sound and the Futy* Critical Edition [New York: Norton Critical Edition, 1987], p. 238); and "just as the mother might feel for the child" (James B. Meriwether and Michael Millgate, eds., *Lion in the Garden: Interviews with William Faulkner: 1926–1962* [Lincoln: University of Nebraska Press, 1980], p. 146). How we have even directed the limits of Caddy as a maternal figure reveals the compulsory nature of motherhood in patriarchy. Over and over, in the criticism of *The Sound and the Fury,* we see Caddy praised as a nurturer to her brothers, most especially Benjy, Mrs. Compson reviled for her failings, and Caddy caught between her role as banished daughter and abandoner of her own daughter.

23 In Irigaray's " 'Frenchwomen,' Stop Trying" (*This Sex,* pp. 198–204), she urgently and impishly counsels perversity as a strategy against the repetition of the same: "Don't even go looking for that alibi. Do what comes to mind, do what you like: without 'reasons,' without 'valid motives,' without 'justification.' You don't have to raise your impulses to the lofty status of categorical imperatives" (p. 203). In the interest of genuinely trying for a new reading, and reading in the spirit of Irigaray's agenda, I offer this alternative title. Since the Appendix has come and

gone, been an introduction and a conclusion, tampering with the title can only be seen as a daring and manly editorial prerogative. I have additionally revalued each of the sections by a date or allusion to identity that emphasizes the female persona that will focus my observations as I work my way through a book whose very design makes all efforts to structure analysis seem doomed. The unwieldiness, rather seepages, of time and character have led me to some ruthless and woefully brief examples of the contradictions I hope to expose.

In rejecting the assumptions about mothers and sons that skew reading experiences of *The Sound and the Fury*, I offer an alternative lens for thinking about the work. I would like to make a case here for disunity, disunity rooted neither in technical experiment, nor in service of theme. In isolation, each section can be explored with a different set of priorities. And the possibility of a different set of priorities emerges. In the radical separation of stories, the female figures achieve different status, even a kind of parity. Caddy and her mother dominate Benjy's story, but without the charged evidence against them brought by Quentin and Jason the possibility of seeing them anew exists. The same is true for each of the other sections. And the particular gain that emerges is that in the final section where Caddy has been reduced to "caddie" (*SF*, p. 315) and as a way for Luster to torment Ben, we have permission to not force the "narrative" to emphasize a role she does not play.

24 See Noel Polk's " 'The Dungeon Was Mother Herself': William Faulkner 1927–31," in *New Directions in Faulkner Studies, 1983* (Doreen Fowler and Ann J. Abadie, eds. [Jackson: University Press of Mississippi, 1983], pp. 61–93) for its stunning distillation of Freudian currents emerging from this creative period.

25 Sally Page, *Faulkner's Women: Characterization and Meaning* (Deland, FL: Everett/Edwards, 1972), p. 65.

26 Philip Weinstein, " 'If I Could Say Mother': Construing the Unsayable about Faulknerian Maternity," in *Faulkner's Discourse: An International Symposium*, ed. Lothar Hönninghausen (Tubingen: Niemeyer, 1989), p. 6.

27 Linda W. Wagner, "Language and Act: Caddy Compson," *Southern Literary Journal* 14.2 (1982): 60–1.

28 Ibid., 52.

29 M. D. Faber, "Faulkner's *The Sound and the Fury:* Object Relations and Narrative Structure," *American Imago* 34.4 (1977): 341.

30 Walter Brylowski, *Faulkner's Olympian Laugh* (Detroit: Wayne State University Press, 1968), p. 67.

31 See Weinstein, "If," and Polk, "Mother." Philip Weinstein charges in ostensibly to clarify the "punitive" portrait of Caroline Compson and to examine the model that "underlies" Faulkner's depiction of a woman whose culture offers her no viable scripts save that of "virginal flirtation and post-maternal complaint" (pp. 3–4). But in short order, Weinstein's "understanding" has yielded this version of Mrs. Compson, who serves as the "ideological monster" of the text (p. 5): "Refusing to be a wife, Caroline Bascomb refuses to be a mother, and Caddy must therefore – and fatally – play that role for her brothers" (p. 4). Such grim rescuing makes one rather pine for abandonment.

32 William Faulkner, *Collected Stories of William Faulkner* (New York: Vintage, 1977), p. 294.

33 Joseph Blotner, *Faulkner: A Biography* (New York: Random House, 1974), vol. 1, pp. 79–80; vol. 2, pp. 1761–2.

34 Irigaray, *This Sex,* p. 84.

35 Joan Williams, "In Defense of Caroline Compson," in *Critical Essays on William Faulkner: The Compson Family,* ed., Arthur Kinney (Boston: G.K. Hall, 1982), pp. 402–7. Although I think Williams is perhaps more generous than the text can fully support, I think it is crucial to note that she alone of *SF* commentators is not "in the business" and perhaps her resistance to the orthodoxy is the result.

Joan Williams has offered a vigorous defense based on the realistic complications in Caroline Compson's life. She counters the critical savagery by noting ways in which Mrs. Compson is a victim of her times and credits Mrs. Compson for the possibilities of nurture, however diminished. She discounts Damuddy's role as gentle model in the family, since there is no textual evidence, save the report she has spoiled Jason, of Damuddy interacting at all. Williams lays blame for the failed marriage at the feet of the head of the household, and reinterprets positively most of the gestures for which Mrs. Compson has been reviled. She sees Mrs. Compson trying to save Caddy's reputation with marriage (a response appropriate to the times); Williams shrewdly suggests that Caddy's confidence in her mother makes possible the trip to French Lick and the marriage, albeit brief, to Herbert Head. Caddy's response to Quentin "that she has to marry someone" appears matter-of-fact; it is Quentin who is obsessed by this tragedy. Williams's Caroline is struggling, beleaguered, and limited, but entirely understandable in her flaws.

36 Gwynn and Blotner, *Faulkner in the University,* p. 1.

37 What to do with women who did not conform to conventional expectations for them was a particularly plaguing problem for modernists

like Faulkner and his contemporary, Hemingway. The "lost Caddy" came back to haunt Faulkner and his readers in the Appendix where she is affiliated with Nazism and Hollywood, serving as either a touchstone or the apotheosis of beauty defiled. Hemingway's decision to have Catherine die in childbirth offers an interesting gloss and alternative to horrific exile. Hemingway's Frederick Henry reflects on Catherine's stoic and sacrificing courage. He says "If people bring so much courage to this world the world has to kill them to break them, so of course it kills them. The world breaks every one and afterward many are strong at the broken places. But those that will not break it kills. It kills the very good and the very gentle and the very brave impartially. If you are none of these you can be sure it will kill you too but there will be no special hurry" (*A Farewell to Arms* [New York: Scribner's 1969], p. 249).

38 Sundquist, *Faulkner*, p. 10.

39 I should like carefully to distinguish my position on Caddy here from the very provocative analysis offered by Minrose Gwin in her *The Feminine and Faulkner Reading (Beyond) Sexual Difference* (Knoxville: University of Tennessee Press, 1990). Unlike Gwin, I do not believe that Caddy is a product of "Faulkner's bisexual artistic (un)consciousness" (p. 37), and I particularly oppose the notion that we are privy to Caddy's voice as it speaks out of "maternal space" of Caddy created in Benjy's discourse (p. 41), or that she exists in Quentin's memory as voiceless. Though Gwin and I share several points of contact, most especially Irigaray's interpretations of female sexuality, we are critically divided in a variety of ways not the least of which is the implications of Caddy's multiplicity. Gwin believes that Caddy is "the text which speaks multiplicity, maternity, sexuality" (46) and that these powers challenge the "pretensions" of unified truth within the patriarchy. I maintain that Caddy is not multivocal so much as she is multiple as a construction, and that the consequences are felt in the genre. If *The Sound and the Fury* can be seen as "other" than a novel, as discrete units with shared elements, the work's claims to aesthetic originality are far greater than we have permitted it in our domestication of it. Furthermore, disunifying Caddy, Mrs. Compson, and even Quentin disrupts habits of reading that reduce female difference to single, same, recognizable shapes. It is particularly interesting to note that Gwin's readings of Caddy's roles in *The Sound and the Fury* deal exclusively with her in relation to males. I'm looking at character variances that point to mother-daughter identities submerged in the work.

40 Minrose C. Gwin, "Feminism and Faulkner: Second Thoughts or, What's a radical feminist doing with a canonical male text anyway?" *Faulkner Journal* 4.1–2 (1988/1989): 55–65.

41 Faber, "Faulkner's *The Sound and the Fury*," 327.

42 I refer here to the historical sleight of hand built on paradox: What you witness, suspect, is only an illusion. If women exercise no power, it is merely an advantage since they are spared the burdens of exercising power. In this case, we have been asked to see Caddy's exclusion of narration as an advantage, since we in theory know her better than if she were allowed to tell her own story. There is a rich and varied literature about the mechanisms and dynamics of power aimed at excluding women from power and authority, and justifying these oppressive practices in the name of consideration – "for her own good." See Marilyn French, *Beyond Power* (New York: Random House, 1985); Elizabeth Janeway, *Powers of the Weak* (New York: Knopf, 1980); and Susan Faludi, *Backlash* (New York: Crown, 1991).

43 See Polk, Weinstein, Bleikasten, and all the sad generations seeking water (*SF*, p. 173).

44 See Lynn Sukenik quoted in Rich, *Of Woman Born*, p. 237.

45 Rich, *Of Woman Born*, p. 223.

46 "Drouth" ["Dry September"]. *William Faulkner Manuscripts 9: These 13*. Introduced and arranged by Noel Polk. (New York: Garland, 1987), p. 246.

47 Rich, *Of Woman Born*, p. 259.

48 Irigaray, *This Sex*, p. 84.

49 Ibid., p. 119.

50 Margaret Whitford, *Luce Irigaray: Philosophy in the Feminine* (London: Routledge, 1991), pp. 111–19.

51 Whitford's efforts to clarify Irigaray's views of the feminine imaginary are pertinent: "Irigaray suggests that symbolizing the mother/daughter relationship, creating *externally located* and *durable* representations of this prototypical relation between women, is an urgent necessity, if women are ever to achieve ontological status in this society" (Margaret Whitford, "Rereading Irigaray," (120) in *Between Feminism and Psychoanalysis*, ed., Teresa Brennan [New York: Routledge and Kegan Paul, 1989], pp. 106–26).

Despite her extreme reduction to commodity in Jason's world and her capitulation to this role, despite her childlessness, Quentin has the potential for functioning as mother. She is circulated and valued in the masculine imaginary as all women are – as products and for productivity. She has economic value because of her womb.

52 A rich body of work has emerged on this subject. Marianne Hirsch, *The Mother/Daughter Plot: Narrative, Psychoanalysis, Feminism* (Bloomington: Indiana University Press, 1989); E. Ann Kaplan, *Motherhood and Representation in Literature and Film, 1830–1960* (New York: Routledge, 1989); and others have come out with psychological and social studies that supplement the works of Nancy Chodorow, *The Reproduction of Mothering: Psychoanalysis and the Sociology of Gender* (Berkeley: University of California Press, 1978); Carol Gilligan, *In a Different Voice: Psychological Theory and Women's Development* (Cambridge University Press, 1982); and Jane Gallop, *The Daughter's Seduction* (Ithaca: Cornell University Press, 1982).

53 Though I disagree with Lester's position that "the individual sections of *The Sound and the Fury* are not intelligible in themselves, [and that] readings of this novel depend on the complex interplay between the sections" ("From Place," p. 141), I endorse her overarching thesis which persuasively concludes that readers of *The Sound and the Fury* have managed to "evade numerous crises of uncertainty" (143).

54 See John Earl Bassett, "Family Conflict in *The Sound and the Fury*," in *Critical Essays*, ed. Arthur Kinney, pp. 408–24; André Bleikasten, *The Most Splendid Failure: Faulkner's The Sound and the Fury* (Bloomington: Indiana University Press, 1976); Mimi Gladstein, "Mothers and Daughters in Endless Procession: Faulkner's Use of the Demeter Persephone Myth," in *Faulkner and Women: Faulkner and Yoknapatawpha, 1985*, Doreen Fowler and Ann J. Abadie, eds. (Jackson: University Press of Mississippi, 1985), pp. 100–12; and John L. Longley, Jr., " 'Who Never Had a Sister': A Reading of *The Sound and the Fury*," in *The Novels of William Faulkner*, ed. R. G. Collings and Kenneth McRobbie (Winnipeg: University of Manitoba Press, 1973), pp. 36–42, for more generous readings wherein Quentin is employed either to highlight the bleakness of the Compson world in 1928, and/or to demonstrate the effect of Caddy's abandonment/exile on her daughter. She is not mentioned in Gwin's *The Feminine and Faulkner*, in Peter Swiggart's *The Art of Faulkner's Novels*, or in *Reading Faulkner* by Wesley Morris with Barbara Alverson Morris, and she appears only twice in *Faulkner and Women*.

55 Irigaray, *This Sex*, pp. 84–5.

56 Ibid., pp. 84–6.

57 See John T. Matthews, *The Play of Faulkner's Language* (Ithaca: Cornell University Press, 1982) for an extensive reading of the economy of loss, especially as captured in Jason's negotiations (pp. 91–103).

58 Irigaray, *This Sex*, pp. 84–5.

59 Irigaray has called for "an examination of the *operation of the 'grammar'* of each figure of discourse, its syntactic laws or requirements, its imaginary configurations, its metaphoric networks, and also, of course, what it does not articulate at the level of utterance: *its silences*" (*This Sex,* p. 75). Part of the work Irigaray feels is necessary to change the forms and contents of the discourses requires a rejection of the programmed universals and a rethinking of "gender/genre" (*This Sex,* p. 102).

60 Cleanth Brooks, *William Faulkner: The Yoknapatawpha Country* (New Haven: Yale University Press, 1966), pp. 339–40.

61 Philip Weinstein credits Jim Hinkle for supplying this information (" 'If,' " p. 4) and Calvin Brown, *A Glossary of Faulkner's South* (New Haven: Yale University Press, 1971) provides a full history for the Merry Widow contraceptive (p. 19). Though we know the Merry Widows on the lid were named Agnes, Mable, Becky, we do not know for a fact if the shiny object discovered by the red-tie man is sealed, or only the lid, or to whom it belongs, and if the sexual partner was Quentin.

62 Irigaray, *This Sex,* p. 84.

63 Bleikasten, *Most Splendid Failure,* p. 158.

64 Irigaray, *This Sex,* p. 84.

65 Irigaray claims that women are denied "the right to speak and to participate in exchange." "Commodities . . . do not take themselves to market on their own; and if they could talk . . . " (*This Sex,* p. 84). If she is correct, then the denial of voice to Caddy (and her daughter) makes a thirteenth way of looking at a blackbird which is far more pernicious than most critics have been inclined to charge.

66 Quentin's revolt and reclamation of her money represents an extraordinary resistance to the solid economy (*This Sex,* pp. 107–9), and manages, I think, to subvert the solid claim on truth, rationality, and "the production of a truth and of a meaning that are excessively univocal" (*This Sex,* p. 78).

67 Ibid., p. 79.

68 Ibid., p. 101.

69 Ibid., p. 157.

70 Ibid., p. 158.

71 Ibid., p. 77.

72 Margaret Atwood imagines an "Underground Frailroad" (*The Handmaid's Tale* [New York: Ballantine, 1987], p. 381) as a resistance movement opposing the subjugation of women held in the reproductively fascist dystopia, Gilead, the setting for Atwood's novel. It

was a network that provided safe stops for Gileadean handmaids and others who sought to regain self-determination.

73 Hélène Vivienne Wenzel, "Introduction to Luce Irigaray's 'And the One Doesn't Stir without the Other,' " *Signs* 7.1 (1981): 56–9. In her "One Doesn't Stir without the Other," Irigaray imagines the possibilities for women other than "mothering" with its attendant grief and resentment. This essay is the companion piece to "This Sex Which Is Not One," and ends with speculations on movement: "And the one doesn't stir without the other. But we do not move together" ("One Doesn't," 67). She specifically looks for connections between mother and daughter which do not require the mother to die to the daughter in the process of giving her life. I mention here a particularly Faulknerian locution in this essay which may bridge the gap between French feminist theory and Yoknapatawpha in ways that discourse never could: "But forgetfulness remembers itself when its memorial disappears" ("One Doesn't," 65).

74 Irigaray, *This Sex*, p. 101. In Irigaray's philosophical efforts to release women from their immobilization by "truth" in the solid economy, she confronts the potential dangers of reappropriation by women who attempt to resist and jam the dominant discourse and its laws (*This Sex*, pp. 68–85). In a fatally cohesive system, where woman's existence is synonymous with the function of Other, Irigaray notes the impossibility for the Other to have an Other: "The impossible 'self-affection' of the Other by itself – of the other by herself? – would be the condition making it possible for any subject to form his/her/its desires" (p. 101). One way Irigaray imagines for the disruption to take place is through a "leap, necessarily ek-static." Such a leap would permit the Other to position oneself "elsewhere," in a realm entirely outside the static discourse that has confined women. In escaping the sameness, the repetition, the systematicity, the sex which is not one can begin to move toward different destinations – self-determined, free to express her own desires and pleasure.

75 Whitford, "Rereading," pp. 117–18.

76 Irigaray, *This Sex*, p. 166.

77 Though it is tempting to focus on Caddy and her life beyond the borders of Mississippi, I would like to pursue the implications of Irigaray's analysis by examining here what the recognition of mother/daughter relationship means for women, its potential for sorority. With the creation of Melissa Meek and the shared school days, we glimpse for the first time female friendship in "our heart's darling." We have been drenched in the masculine constructions of sisterhood,

the Little Sister Death of Quentin's section, but in the Appendix for the first time we witness active female to female care tied not to family or duty, but out of sheer concern and affection. This section throws into stark relief how bereft the female community has been – why does Mrs. Compson not mention other mothers, and whom does Miss Quentin play with? Where are the little girls in Jefferson that are not merely objects of Benjy's observations at the gate? Melissa Meek brings home how profoundly absent girl friends are to the world of *The Sound and the Fury.* Susan Donaldson ("Rereading Faulkner Rereading Cowley: Authority and Gender in the Compson Appendix" [unpublished essay] deepens the sense of exception in this section of the Appendix when she notes that it contains a pointedly present tense embedded narrative. When this detail is considered in conjunction with the utterly mobile, entirely fluid status of the Appendix as a document – put it first, put it last, take it out – I would suggest it is indeed a happy marriage of fluid economies. Given the mobility of the Appendix and Faulkner's belief in it as "the key" to the whole book, I see authorization for Irigarayan method. If the Appendix is a key, then it unlocks the truth about the work, reminding us that this novel need not be one, that readings of it should not be one either.

78 Jason's response to Melissa's appeal that he recognize Caddy fulfills the patriarchal prescription of sameness: "Dont make me laugh. This bitch aint thirty yet. The other one's fifty now" (*SF,* p. 340). Despite Melissa's attempt to *disrupt,* Jason acts out of the power of domination and its ability to *"reduce all others to the economy of the Same"* (*This Sex,* p. 74). Caddy has never been other than bitch, and the "different" woman in the photo is the same bitch as well.

3

"Now I Can Write": Faulkner's Novel of Invention

DONALD M. KARTIGANER

THE NATURE of the superior text is to resist its readings: to complicate, at some crucial turn in the interpretive process, the categories and conventions that have formed a reader's bridge into that text, without which the act of interpretation cannot begin. Although selected in part on the basis of the cursory views that tell us quickly the outlines and major conflicts of a text, essentially these conventions constitute what we are and know *prior* to reading. They may be public or private, the shared literary and sociopolitical history of a community of readers, or the more personal history of a particular reader. They may steer a reading to an apparent center of the text or toward its margins, may refer to a largely concealed system of meaning governing the text and our responses to it – what some call its "ideology" – or discover a subversive system that clashes with that meaning.

These approaches may claim or unconsciously imply either their power or their powerlessness, a position authorized by the prevailing value system or victimized by it, but they are all strategies of reading. Their object is the traditional one of familiarizing the text, even if that process of familiarization discloses a structure of oppression. The strategies prepare a system of signs, a critical language, through which the text assumes meaning. This meaning, however, has been largely predetermined by the strategies. Reading thus necessarily projects a text known primarily through what is *already* known, preventing it from expanding beyond the boundaries of the approach adopted at the outset. Reading produces no new knowledge but only confirmation and extension of its own origins.

Inferior texts are written to cater to such readings, good texts to undo them. At some stage of the interaction between the good text and the good reader a disruption begins to take place, as the text threatens to violate the interpretive scheme being brought to bear on it. The text, speaking necessarily *through* the critical language of the reading – it has no other way to communicate with the reader – begins to utter what that language has not only not wished to hear, but did not think could be spoken within its vocabulary. Somehow, text and reader confront the unexpected possibilities of their engagement, the meanings neither could speak prior to their meeting. Strategy begins to unravel: the comic encounters its sorrow, romance its realism, honor its shame, revolution its reactionary shadow.

This dynamic of surprise is not merely the intrusion of a deconstructive mode that discloses the repressed desire of every conscious thought, substituting for predetermined meaning meaning perpetually postponed by the revelation of ambiguity. Although a readiness to deconstruct whatever is in place is crucial to the genuine reading engagement, it is but the prelude to new meaning: the meaning whose possibility now exists, supplanting others, which neither text nor reader nor reading has previously known.[1]

In terms of this reading process, as in so many other ways, *The Sound and the Fury* has a unique place in the Faulkner canon and a distinctive one in modern literature generally. For it is a novel which carries its resistance to the most extreme end this side of incoherence. Its principal object is that it *should not be read,* in the sense that it seeks to withstand from beginning to end every critical strategy. To put this in a more positive way, *The Sound and the Fury* fiercely celebrates invention, the freedom of a prose that communicates yet will not be controlled into what normally passes for a stable set of meanings. The novel insists, clinging to the letter of its borrowed title, on "signifying nothing" – a nothing that is neither chaos nor philosophical nihilism, but rather the projection of a profundity that lies within its words and yet looms beyond what we can claim as our comprehension.

This is a potentially damaging assertion, seeming to equate the significant with the obscure, as if the novel, in the terms F. R. Leavis once used to criticize Conrad's *Heart of Darkness,* were "intent on making a virtue out of not knowing what [it] means."[2]

Perhaps it is more accurate to say that *The Sound and the Fury*, like comparable texts such as *Heart of Darkness* and *The Waste Land*, is trying to make a virtue out of knowing *more* than it means, trying to force language to reach beyond the meanings that precede and prepare it. In the pathetic terms of the idiot Benjy, it is "trying to say" a desire lacking an available language, but which is neither unreal nor insignificant. Its quest is the speech that says what is as yet not only unsaid but unsayable. Reading *The Sound and the Fury* thus becomes an experience of persistent contradiction with regard to the *degree* of understanding we achieve and to the *kind* of understanding, its value and implication.

Does *The Sound and the Fury have* meaning? On the one hand we come away from the novel with the sense that we have witnessed, through a difficult yet powerfully moving and detailed prose, the tragic decline of a once prominent family in the early twentieth-century South. On the other hand, we cannot escape the nagging sense of cognitive defeat, of having witnessed a series of calamities whose necessity and cause keep eluding us, of our inability to read comprehensively the tale that has been so strikingly told.

And what *kind* of meaning, if meaning there is? We encounter a family stricken into a paralysis of alcoholism and hypochondria, idiocy and neurosis, promiscuity and futile if not pointless theft – and yet this paralysis discovers its history to us in a style and structure of narrative revolution. The Compsons' bereavement over lost innocence, lost honor, lost job becomes the vibrant prose of breakthrough. The paradox is not simply a conflict between form and content; the Compson monologues individually, the novel as a whole – including its "traditional" concluding section – register their sorrow and their confusion as an ecstatic anguish that excites even as it saddens.

The effect is that of an equivalence always awry, like a slant rhyme grinding with tension, or a fugue in which an identical melody is being played in major and minor keys. Freedom and entrapment, obsessive reminiscence and defiance of all norms, despair and exhilaration, employ the same words to totally different ends. The novel reads as a narrative always beginning, opening to new configurations of meaning, *and* a narrative turning perpetually backward, looking to the past to conclude the process of meaning.

The Sound and the Fury invokes this set of warring emotions because of its deep commitment to invention, to the creation of a text that more than anything else seeks to *be itself,* not the reflection of what we and our strategies of reading require it to be. It seeks the status of an original text, a quest that imposes the double action of mourning what it no longer can depend on and proclaiming the fact of its freedom. It declares what it *is* in the wake of what it is *not.*

Writing *The Sound and the Fury*

When in 1933 Faulkner wrote several drafts of an introduction to a new edition of *The Sound and the Fury* planned by Random House but later abandoned, he remembered the writing of the novel as the crucial moment in his career. Its inception and the process of its development became at least in memory the defining circumstances of his great creative leap forward. The result was a novel unlike anything he had ever written, with an effect on him unlike that of anything he would ever write: a novel of and about invention.

The Sound and the Fury was a radical departure from Faulkner's previous work, in part because it had to be – written, as it were, on the rebound from the rejection of *Flags in the Dust* by Boni and Liveright, the publisher of his first two novels. Faulkner's high estimation of *Flags,* which was both his initial foray into the world of Yoknapatawpha and his first major use of the Falkner family history, is evident in the letter he wrote to Liveright soon after its completion in September 1927: "I have written THE book, of which those other things were but foals. I believe it is the damdest best book you'll look at this year, and any other publisher."[3] Horace Liveright's reply over a month later must have stunned Faulkner: "It is with sorrow in my heart that I write to tell you that three of us have read Flags in the Dust and don't believe that Boni and Liveright should publish it. Furthermore, as a firm deeply interested in your work, we don't believe that you should offer it for publication. . . . It is diffuse and non-integral with neither very much plot development nor character development. . . . The story really doesn't get anywhere and has a thousand loose ends."[4]

Although, after eleven rejections, he subsequently allowed his friend Ben Wasson to cut *Flags* into the book published as *Sartoris,* Faulkner's response was not to take Liveright's criticisms at face value, to write a more orderly, integrated novel, with no "loose ends." Rather, as he recalled in 1933, he chose to alter his whole approach to the task of writing itself, his relationship to literary history and to the demands of publishers, revising his understanding of the meaning and function of literary criteria.

"One day," he wrote, "I seemed to shut a door between me and all publishers' addresses and book lists"[5] – as if he were done with the very idea of publication. He also claimed that, in the process of writing *The Sound and the Fury,* he had come to the end of reading.

> I discovered then that I had gone through all that I had ever read, from Henry James through Henty to newspaper murders, without making any distinction or digesting any of it, as a moth or a goat might. After The Sound and the Fury and without needing to open another book and in a series of delayed repercussions like summer thunder, I discovered the Flauberts and Dostoievskys and Conrads whose books I had read ten years ago. With The Sound and the Fury I learned to read and quit reading, since I have read nothing since.

Having abandoned publishers and on the verge of abandoning books, possibly even readers, "I said to myself, Now I can write. Now I can just write."[6]

In recounting the great shift of his career in terms of a flight from publishers' lists and books, Faulkner laid a groundwork for a reading of *The Sound and the Fury* as a leap toward autonomy: a shaking off of that whole world of literary history that exists prior to writing and of publishers and readers who wait to judge its outcome, that world already fixed with meaning and value, whose languages he had read and reread, and which now, having brought him to the brink of original speech, threatened to bind him to reiteration.

His recollection of the beginnings of the novel continues the emphasis on the sheer freedom of the experience. "When I began it I had no plan at all. I wasn't even writing a book. I was thinking of books, publication, only in the reverse, in saying to myself, I wont have to worry about publishers liking or not liking this at all." This statement eventually leads Faulkner to the most remarkable sentence of all: "So I, who had never had a sister and was fated to lose my daughter in infancy [1931], set out to make myself a beautiful and tragic little girl." The claims of independence – no plan, no publisher, the discovery of the end of reading – climax abruptly on an image of pure invention. From that which was *not,* not before and – seen retroactively – not after, I will make something. It is as if the creation of Caddy were *ab ovo:* a replica of nothing outside the text, just as inside the text she lives solely as the creation of her three brothers, who in Faulkner's memory strangely *precede* her: "Caddy had three brothers *almost before* I wrote her name on paper" (my emphasis).

In his memory of her role in the writing of the novel Faulkner elevated Caddy to a figure for the novel itself. In later years the two would become virtually interchangeable objects of affection. Of Caddy: "To me she was the beautiful one, she was my heart's darling. That's what I wrote the book about."[7] Of *The Sound and the Fury:* "That's the one that's my – I consider the best, not – well, best is the wrong word – that's the one that I love the most."[8] Caddy is not so much a character in the novel as the embodiment of its whole dynamic, not origin but the retroactively conceived occasion of its vague desires. The text revolves around her possible image – like the possible unity of its four perspectives – yet she is neither defined by that text nor "reduced" to "telling what was going on."[9]

Like Caddy, *The Sound and the Fury* remained for Faulkner the novel independent of prior determinations, full of telling yet never to be told. His frequent descriptions of it as a succession of narrative "failures" were also assertions of its triumph in sustaining its radical originality. The writer's inability to complete a narrative of his own conception confirms the power of that conception to drive the text beyond all the temptations of centering, beyond the "reductions" of resolution. It practices the rare eloquence of "signifying nothing."

Reading *The Sound and the Fury*

How then do we read *The Sound and the Fury?* What are the implications for interpretation of a novel whose very resistance to reading seems to be, as Wallace Stevens would put it, the "cry of its occasion"? Each of the four sections of the text situates itself in a verbal universe of its own, characterized by a predominant focus on one period of development: childhood, adolescence, adulthood; a literary mode which it simultaneously emulates and parodies; and a form of mental movement and continuity that guides the peculiar logic of its associations. Common to all the sections is their utter remoteness from each other and their freedom from any criteria by which the validity of their perspectives may be measured. Each narrative consumes a day in the life of the Compson family and its offspring, yet none of them either corroborates or refutes the others. Rather they all stand as independent renderings of a history which is virtually being invented anew in each rendering. Consequently, the novel provides no means of gauging the "correctness" of its four perspectives. There is no single source among the four that we have grounds for judging as more reliable than the others; nor is there any possible collation of the whole history – a fifth blackbird – that is larger and more valid than the sum of its fragmented parts.[10]

Each narrative repeats the radical commitment to invention Faulkner describes in his 1933 introduction, creating out of the sister it "never had," out of a sense of *something absent,* a version of what it needs to complete its world. And like his own experience of writing the novel as he remembered it, the method of each is to seal that world off from the weight of all previous words and the realities they allege, from everything that constitutes and judges, that seeks to bind consciousness and utterance to the rock of some form of repetition.

Yet whatever the obsession with originality, language and historical and literary inheritance make borrowers of us all, and Faulkner's four attempts to bring to plausible life what had no prior existence dip necessarily into what he called the "lumber room" or the "filing case" or the "junk box" of his reading and listening and seeing.[11] In this, his first truly experimental text, much of the "lumber room" contents consist of the literary modes and movements available to him in 1928, and still available to us as readers: rhetorical avenues of entrance that allow us – as they allowed Faulkner's four narrators – to take temporary hold of the absence at the core of each narrative. In each of the four sections there is a dominant literary mode which Faulkner employs but always with the parodic twist that transforms it into his own unique expression. The double-edged implementation of these modes evokes our own double-edged response of recognition and estrangement, as we find ourselves compelled by a series of recreated worlds which we can neither reject nor unequivocally accept.

The literary mode Faulkner used most exhaustively is the stream of consciousness method of the first three sections of the novel, already brought to something like definitiveness by James Joyce in *Ulysses.* In his *Introduction to Metaphysics,* translated into English by T. E. Hulme in 1912, a book Faulkner might well have read, Henri Bergson pointed to the stream of consciousness as an example of fictional narrative that attempts to grasp personality from within rather than from without, no longer enumerating "traits of . . . character" but bringing the reader into an identification "with the person of the hero himself." The result – a version of the substitution of intuition for intellect that Bergson believed necessary for the authentic perception of reality – is an experience of reading that abandons the "description, history, and analysis [of] the relative" for that "coincidence with the person himself [that] . . . alone give[s] me the absolute."[12]

Faulkner's crucial distortion of Bergson, and of Joyce, is that the characters we identify with in *The Sound and the Fury* and the reality of what their "absolutely" perceived consciousnesses register are indelibly marked by their mental derangement. By extending what is already a major narrative innovation emphasizing individuality of character into the further uniqueness of the unbalanced mind, the Compson monologues perform a parody of stream of consciousness, inviting the reader to possess the absolute by coinciding with three types of madness. The result is an intensified originality of form – achieved within the practice of a derived mode – and an intensified originality of vision. Benjy, Quentin, and Jason project worlds that cannot reflect anything we can conceivably recognize as the real (unlike the consciousnesses of Joyce's Stephen, Bloom, and Molly), but rather, in Mr. Compson's words, implement desires in forms "symmetrical above the flesh"[13] – accountable to nothing except the needs of their crazed imaginations.

The novel's revision of the stream of consciousness technique is the model of each section's dynamic of appropriation and parody, dependency and originality. Each narrative voice pursues an autonomous tale that risks being neither more nor less than *unlikeness:* telling what it has never quite known, yet recreating undeniable, if unverifiable, truth.

Benjy

Benjy's monologue is presumably the one Faulkner wrote in the initial burst of freedom he referred to in his 1933 introduction. Benjy's mind moves through the world and time wholly without a controlling perspective, voicing a prose of pure presentation. Things seem to reveal themselves of their own accord, unchosen, uncontrived, as if to an innocent eye unwilling or unable to impose any imaginative pressure on them, any prior models of ordering or cultural bias. Benjy can feel joy and sorrow, and he holds fiercely, as we shall see, to the particular value of constancy. But the narrative movement is that of a mind utterly open to whatever sights and sounds and smells happen to touch its senses, impelled by them to some association forward or backward in time. The appearance of a nail, a carriage, a gate, a spoken name or phrase, a particular physical movement or gesture – each triggers an echo somewhere within the span of Benjy's thirty-three years, instantly unfolding, through no act of will on his part, as the next moment of his freewheeling mind.

Benjy's idiocy bestows on him the quality of being without memory. He *recognizes* nothing through the lens of intervening time, whether it be minutes or years, but knows always with the freshness of a first encounter. He *relives* each moment rather than remembering it and so perceives it not as the repetition it actually is but, Adamically, as the first and only moment of all. Yet the price of his idiocy is that, for all his apparent freedom from preconception, he remains wholly trapped within the links of his finite chain of forgotten moments. Each "new" experience plays within a tight circumference of eternal return, remaking pure unpredictability into pure duplication.

Benjy's severely objective, concrete, unornamented prose resembles the Imagist movement in early twentieth-century poetry, with its familiar credo of the "direct treatment of the 'thing.' " The aim of the Imagist, according to Pound, was to "present an intellectual and emotional complex in an instant of time . . . which gives that sense of sudden liberation; that sense of freedom from time limits and space limits."[14] Free from the superfluous word, from abstraction and moralizing commentary, the poem achieves what Hugh Kenner summarizes as a "sculptured stasis."[15]

Benjy's sharply edged scenes, again and again rendering the Compsons in a striking, seemingly absolute simplicity, read like a series of Imagist poems:

> *Then he went to the window and looked out. He came back and took my arm. Here she come, he said. Be quiet, now. We went to the window and looked out. It came out of Quentin's window and climbed across into the tree. We watched the tree shaking. The shaking went down the tree, then it came out and we watched it go away across the grass. Then we couldn't see it.* (74)

Benjy's eye grants the scene an absolute integrity. He does not transform the "it," obscurely seen, into the identity of Caddy's daughter, but allows her to remain a shape. Hidden by the leaves, she proceeds down the tree as motion, a "shaking." Reemerging, but still only a shape, "it" disappears across the grass. The idiot's eye sees with such precision and with such freedom from assumption, its literal language reads to *us* as metaphor: "*shaking went down the tree.*"

The brilliance of the image, however, cannot help but parody its model, and thus achieve a certain distinction within its derived form, if only by the source of the vision in the mind of Benjy Compson. The aims of the Imagists, to achieve a condition of language in which "words so raised by prosody to attention assert themselves *as words,* and make a numinous claim on our attention," were not supposed to be met by the mind of an idiot.[16] More important, the numinous word in Benjy's monologue projects not merely the "sculptured stasis" of a caught moment, but an entire *world* of stasis, of people frozen in the unchanging posture, endlessly repeated, which has become for Benjy the particular norm of their identity: Mother ill, Father detached, Quentin distressed over some breach in custom, Jason isolated, tattling.

Caddy is the only example of change in Benjy's monologue, and her portrayal reveals most emphatically the static effect of his unpremeditated narrative. He constantly represents her in what is for him the terror of transition, threatening to expand out of some prior identity: wearing perfume, kissing Charley in the swing, having had sexual intercourse. Since Benjy's perception is grounded in a principle of exact repetition, he regards transition as an aberration, unnatural – finally an illusion that violates no moral code but the code of reality itself. The thrust of his vision is thus to see Caddy restored to an "innocence" which has nothing to do with morality but is for him simply an original, and genuine, condition.

Sometimes these restorations literally take place: " 'We dont like perfume ourselves.' Caddy said" (43); " 'I wont.' she said. 'I wont anymore, ever. Benjy. Benjy'. . . . Caddy took the kitchen soap and washed her mouth at the sink, hard. Caddy smelled like trees" (48). But the power of the monologue is to project an imaginary restoration that, for all the transitions it registers, finally keeps Caddy in a condition of stasis that is compelling, wonderfully moving, and quite beyond any valid criterion of reality we have. Benjy's Caddy – pure, loving, altruistic – whose variations from that identity take place as temporary deformities, is an identity that cannot possibly exist. She is a projected reality, as false as a handful of stills snatched from the early stages of a decade-long movie.

Caddy can be nothing more or less in Benjy's monologue than its mode of vision, a mode blind to durational process, recording the real in such rigid clarity that Benjy can return to it again and again. Benjy's repeated *is,* invulnerable to forces of change and development, always the same in his inhuman economy, must be for Caddy the eternal *was* of nonexistence, of never having occurred because it always recurs in precisely the same way. Benjy's Caddy is made forever unreal by his capacity to restore her to an essential, unvarying repetition: a past uninflected by the human process of memory.

The monologue proclaims by its stasis the autonomy of its vision; it is less a valid representation than a wish defending itself against truth. Caddy Compson is a sister *no one* ever had, a frozen figure that escapes reality into image. Benjy will always be three years old and his world eternal. His monologue begins in the morning with the cry of a word, "caddie," which he mistakenly believes refers to his missing sister. It concludes, as all the sections do, at the end of the day, but in this case the day is twenty years earlier, with that initial word, "caddie," completed by what was *then* its full signification. For all the movement within the monologue, at its end Caddy is age six, in bed with Benjy, age three, the unchanging fiction of his desire.

Quentin

Quentin's monologue logically follows Benjy's in its emphasis on the adolescent years of the Compson children, but its narrative mode is a complete reversal. Quentin counters the uncontrolled movement of Benjy's narration with the most purposeful and artificially contrived narration in the novel. If Benjy's prose suggests an absolute openness of mind to the sensual thrusts of a real world (however binding within previous experience that openness will prove to be) Quentin's reflects the capacity and willingness of mind to set the real world aside, substituting a fantasized one that repeats it in a finer tone.

"June Second, 1910" secures itself from the outset within the lines of an elaborately prescribed plot: the story of the suicide of Quentin Compson. Quentin wakens to the last day of his life with the details of its beginning and end already intact in his mind, much like the design of the Aristotelian mythos that governs tragedy. From about 7:45 A.M. until 1:00 P.M. Quentin meticulously carries out each of the stages that will end with his death later that evening: notes written to the appropriate parties, clothes packed, library books neatly stacked, two suits laid out, flatirons purchased and safely hidden near a bridge over the Charles River.

Quentin performs these steps with all the aplomb and skill of an experienced actor in a drama. Following a long afternoon interim, he completes the final details, in the penultimate scene of the play, with the same composure: he cleans his now bloodstained vest, changes his tie, collar, and shirt, gets a fresh handkerchief, cleans his teeth, brushes his hat. Exit. The whole sequence has a well rehearsed look, as if Quentin were not so much experiencing the climax of his life as representing it, one step removed from its actual occurrence.

Although beginning and end are in place, however, the middle of this well wrought plot has a curiously random quality. What traditionally should be the gradual unfolding of beginning, through climax, to conclusion remains in Quentin's narrative wholly amorphous, a shapeless space of time. His task during this lengthy phase is not to advance the plot but, on the contrary, to establish the irrelevancy of the middle, of ordinary, unartful time. Quentin wishes to "lose time" (83); or, in both senses of the phrase, to kill time.

And so, for six or seven hours, Quentin wanders, opening himself almost Benjylike to various encounters which, on the face of it, have nothing to do with the suicide plot he has momentarily set aside. Whereas each stage of his preparations has been carried out according to an oblique reference to time – the quarter and half-hour chimes, the hourly whistles he acknowledges yet positions himself not to hear – once his plot is firmly in place, Quentin can forget time, bury it in the "meantime," as irrelevant to the day's significant action. The deliberate purpose of this idleness is for Quentin to effect on his last day a final separation of categories he has previously tried, unsuccessfully, and perhaps only halfheartedly, to integrate: content and form, purpose and gesture, life and art.

Quentin's afternoon of aimless wandering weaves back and forth between present event and past memory, recalled and repeated gestures, in defense of interchangeable women against interchangeable men. The upshot of it all is Quentin's realization of the extent to which the gestures themselves have always held his primary loyalty. As Michael Millgate has written, "Whenever Quentin acts, his concern is for the act's significance as a gesture rather than for its practical efficacy. He seeks pertinaciously for occasions to fight in defence of his sister's honour, knowing in advance that he will be beaten and concerned in retrospect only that he has performed that act in its ritualistic and symbolic aspects."[17]

By the end of the day, Quentin has been beaten up twice and accused of kidnapping. His strange triumph, however, is that "nothing" has happened, his harrowing afternoon is wholly and strategically pointless. It is irrelevant to the suicide plot that surrounds it, exemplifying the difference between what Frank Kermode calls "successive" or "passing time" – *chronos* – and significant time – *kairos* – "charged with a meaning derived from its relation to the end."[18] In his afternoon of remembered and repeated humiliations in the name of honor, Quentin succeeds in confirming the separation of the "reality" of his life from all its gestures, freeing him into the purity of fiction.

He is therefore ready to return to his dormitory room and his plot, to move from passing time to full time. With a grim irony, suicide becomes Quentin's only significant action, the form beyond farce. It is not a means of ending a life still cluttered with reality, but of *replacing* it: of epitomizing a condition of being in which form will not falter.

Quentin's project in "June Second, 1910" is to enact his life as an exemplary version of High Modernism, in which the artist's imagination transforms a mundane reality into its capitalized counterpart, the more authentic Reality. Quentin is the novel's High Modernist voice in his desire to separate himself from normal human activity, particularly sexuality, and to transform life into a comparably isolated and remote art, rid of what we usually mean by reference and relevance, in order to approach some purer version of these: a "radiant truth out of space and time."[19]

But as Benjy parodies the Imagist voice, Quentin parodies his own mode by his neurotic desire not to gain a true vision of life through art, to discover the Truth of truth, but willfully to sunder these pairs, as if they were categories of entirely different worlds. The danger of Modernism is its inclination to push past what Kermode, writing of Yeats, calls its "reconciling images, containing life in death, death in life, movement and stillness, action and contemplation, body and soul,"[20] and enter a realm in which literature not only abandons the quotidian but celebrates its own irrelevance. "Life" becomes an occupation for our servants; or as

Quentin puts it, regarding the sexual identity he would renounce: "O That That's Chinese I dont know Chinese" (116).

Quentin's quest is to produce and occupy a supreme autonomy: a unique language that is, but does not mean. Faulkner's parody of that quest ultimately renders it as a perversion, a deliberately lifeless art that must necessarily be a death-filled one. Paradoxically, his parody is Faulkner's means of loosening Quentin's narrative from its obvious debt, manifesting that impulse of parody toward originality Linda Hutcheon has described: certain parodic texts "actually manage to free themselves from the backgrounded text enough to create a new and autonomous form."[21]

The primary vehicle of Quentin's quest is his sister Caddy, whom he projects as always already fallen into that "reality" which is less than his gestural desire. Unlike Benjy, Quentin has no imaginary vision of a prelapsarian Caddy violated by change: His Caddy – every bit as imaginary – is *originally* "changed": muddied, kissed, fucked, impregnated, *in order to be* redeemed by Quentin himself into a fictionalized enhancement of her condition. He is not seeking to *return* Caddy to a prior state of innocence, for such innocence has never existed in Quentin's mind. Rather, he seeks to exploit what he always insists is Caddy's corruption as the contrast to his unwordly art, to reinvent her *forward* into the partner of his fictions even as her "inherently" flawed identity remains as the enduring sign of his imaginative triumph.

My point is not to deny that Caddy has had a real existence outside Quentin's (and Benjy's and Jason's) imagination – perhaps even some of the normal experiences of a young girl between the ages of six and eighteen – but to emphasize how little of that experience we actually get in this novel, and how much of it is filtered entirely through her brothers' perceptions. Quentin and Benjy are adept at reading relatively harmless scenes (muddy drawers, perfume, kissing) into moral upheavals. As for Caddy's sexual intercourse, what do we know of it?

The deflowering of Caddy by Dalton Ames may be literal truth but it *reads* in Quentin's monologue like a fantasy of Quentin's as much as a romanticization by Caddy of her first lover. There is the very name itself (compare "Herbert Head" and "Gerald Bland"); there are the descriptions whose sources, Caddy or Quentin, are not made specific, "his face so brown his eyes so blue" (92), and those that are, "he looked like he was made out of bronze" (158). Above all, there is the scene on the bridge in which Dalton Ames responds to Quentin's threats with a series of extraordinary gestures: "he . . . rolled a cigarette with those two swift motions spun the match over the rail," catches both Quentin's swinging hands and without aiming his pistol shoots a piece of bark floating away from the bridge for six lines of text, then calmly offers Quentin the pistol ("because youve seen what itll do") so he may take his vengeance (159–61). Dalton Ames is the dream of an adolescent of either sex, unadulterated pulp fiction with "poor Quentin," who has "never done that" (151), as witness. As with Caddy's "corruption," how else but by his own disgrace can Quentin measure the marvelousness of his invention?

Caddy is the ground of Quentin's imagining. If Benjy's is the sister no one ever had, because he inscribes her in Eden, then Quentin's is the sister *everyone* has had whom he distorts into the occasion of his fantasy.

Quentin's most extreme fictionalization of Caddy is his insistence that they have committed incest, that he is her only lover (although, interestingly enough, he does not claim to be the father of her unborn child):

> *we did how can you not know it if youll just wait Ill tell you how it was it was a crime we did a terrible crime it cannot be hid you think it can but wait. . . . Ill tell Father then itll have to be because you love Father then well have to go away amid the pointing and the horror the clean flame Ill make you say we did Im stronger than you Ill make you know we did you thought it was them but it was me listen I fooled you all the time it was me you thought I was in the house.* (148–9)

Quentin vacillates between the attempt to persuade Caddy that they have actually been lovers without her knowing it, and the attempt – even more bizarre – to persuade her to accept the power of the word over the flesh. Quentin is engaged in High Modernist seduction at the furthest reaches of perversion and parody, abandoning the referentiality Modernism seeks to revise and expand. It is neither sex nor hell, the physical nor the metaphysical, that has significance for Quentin but only the formulated words, the pure *saying*, "symmetrical above the flesh" (177). His leap beyond the Modern is his awareness that there is a reality that declares the fiction utterly false. His originality becomes a form of faith, *credo quia absurdum est;* a form of insanity; a form of art fulfilling itself only as willfully irrelevant invention.

Quentin states his need unequivocally in the confession he makes, or perhaps only imagines making, to his father: "and he did you try to make her do it and i i was afraid to i was afraid she might and then it wouldnt have done any good but if i could tell you we did it would have been so and then the others wouldnt be so and then the world would roar away" (177).[22] Quentin's desire is to be in a world where telling alone makes a thing "so," where unreality may be spoken into fact, as happens "when... desires become words" (117).

Caddy's and Mr. Compson's unbelief urges Quentin toward his final fiction. The act of suicide that comprises the essential plot of "June Second, 1910" is his supreme creation, his tour de force, especially in the Faulknerian sense of implying an art more perfectly accomplished than profound. The lack of profundity is exactly the point, for Quentin's final gesture is the triumph of a real action emptying itself of its reality.

The ultimate effect of his methodical implementation of his plans is to transform suicide into a performance-of-suicide. Quentin enacts the end of a life made unendurable by its resistance to preconceived form as a sequence perfectly formed. He plays his role so artfully – he will not break up his lines to weep – as to replace reality at last with illusion, the existential with the aesthetic. Quentin's action is pure gesture ridding death of its mortality, as if death had become so much at one with the performance of it that there is no one living left to die.

Jason

Perhaps the most significant change in The Corrected Text of *The Sound and the Fury* was the decision by its editor, Noel Polk, to omit "Appendix/Compson, 1699–1945," composed by Faulkner in 1945 for *The Portable Faulkner.* Without that latter-day interpretation by Faulkner, with its description of Jason Compson as "The first sane Compson since before Culloden.... Logical rational contained and even a philosopher in the old stoic tradition," Jason assumes, unobstructed, his original characterization as a man not only angry and frustrated, but in fact quite mad.[23]

Jason spends his Good Friday, "April Sixth, 1928," in violent motion, lashing out mentally, orally, and sometimes physically at every person, practice, or institution he believes stands in his way (which includes all), in pursuit of ends so full of contradiction as to be both unrealizable and incomprehensible. He knows neither sense nor self-interest. By the end of his day he has accomplished nothing but motion itself, as if his unwitting goal were neither the past of Benjy, the *was,* nor the future perfect of Quentin, the *will have been,* but a perpetual present, the *now,* of interminable process. Jason's goal is to prolong his tirade against the world: not to effect change, clear a path to some end, a point of rest, but to unleash his inexhaustible rage.

Who is Jason Compson and what does he want? He would ridicule the notion that he cannot say or guess. He assumes that he is a man of sober judgment, of solid practical sense, who with a little cooperation from his family could well achieve his aim of becoming a successful businessman, part of the New South mercantile upper class that has replaced the old planter aristocracy.[24] But this coherent perception of self and ambition, which eighteen years later Faulkner curiously remembered as fact, is compromised and contradicted throughout Jason's monologue.

To begin with, Jason Compson is a terrible businessman, as an employee, as a player in the cotton market, and in the day-to-day handling of his money. His day's work at Earl's store is a sham. Half the time he is simply gone – to the telegraph office, the printing office, home, or into the countryside chasing after his niece Quentin and her boyfriend. On the premises he is virtually worthless, spending the time reading his mail, doctoring checks, arguing with Quentin, and bitterly resenting the few customers he actually waits on. As for the cotton market, although given excellent advice by the "jews" he detests, and in a position to make a handsome profit by selling short in a falling market, he fails to keep close watch and thus misses his opportunity to purchase shares at their lowest value.[25] Though careful to burn two free tickets to the carnival rather than give them to Luster, Jason is a profligate spender: an extra forty dollars to his prostitute Lorraine, a five-dollar tip to the maid at the whorehouse, a refusal to take Earl's offer of a free meal. To top it off, he has withdrawn his mother's thousand-dollar investment for him in Earl's store in order to buy a new car which he claims he doesn't need!

Despite this total irresponsibility toward his employer's interests, his mother's, or his own, Jason blames everyone else for his failures, and even has the nerve to mock Earl for making only eight percent on his business: "Why I could take his business in one year and fix him so he'd never have to work again" (228) – a preposterous claim, given Jason's colossal incompetence. A measure of his economic shrewdness is his angry insistence that the carnival is a liability to the town because of the money spent on it. Resenting the inconvenience it causes him, he entirely misses the fact that Earl's business is booming because of it.

There is more here than ineptness or negligence. Jason spends his day working against himself with manic deliberateness: goading Earl to fire him for his uselessness, pursuing Quentin when he should be watching the cotton market, indiscriminately throwing away money he has been stealing from Caddy (and his family) for fifteen years. As much as he torments others, Jason torments himself most of all, a fact he conceals primarily through his wild-swinging and mordant humor. Everything and everyone are fair game, as he dissolves the pathos and impassioned suffering of his brothers and sister into the coarsest ridicule: "Once a bitch always a bitch, what I say" (180); "I could hear the Great American Gelding snoring away like a planing mill" (263); "I never had university advantages because at Harvard they teach you how to go for a swim at night without knowing how to swim" (196). He includes himself among the objects of his sarcasm: "and then I happened to look around and I had my hand right on a bunch of poison oak. The only thing I couldn't understand was why it was just poison oak and not a snake or something" (241).

What might have been the sign of Jason's sanity, a sharp satire grounded in some stable norm, deflating not only Compson inequity and pretentiousness but our own sentimental readings of the preceding monologues, becomes a fury cut entirely loose from any center of value. Jason is nothing less than a Postmodern voice in the novel, exemplifying in his violent comedy the demolition of ground that the Postmodern derives from a more moderate Modernism that questions and revises ground. Perhaps the most extreme of Faulkner's innovations in this novel, Jason is a mix of Kafka's K. and Lenny Bruce, perpetual victim and master of vituperation, registering universal disruption through the gaiety of black-comic rage. What pushes Jason to the edge of the Postmodern, enabling him to parody what is already a parodic form, is his insistence that despite the chaos around him, he alone occupies a stable, coherent center. He remystifies his own demystifying stance, claims a ground he continually deconstructs through the chain of contradiction running through his monologue. He is the Postmodern blind to the very precariousness that is its meaning and power.

In Jason's shotgun attack, the butt of one joke becomes the norm of the next. "I haven't got much pride," Jason insists, "I cant afford it with a kitchen full of niggers to feed and robbing the state asylum of its star freshman. Blood, I says, governors and generals. It's a dam good thing we never had any kings and presidents; we'd all be down there at Jackson chasing butterflies" (230). But several pages later, Jason speaks of rebuking those who would criticize any Compson: "you dont hear the talk that I hear and you can just bet I shut them up too. I says my people owned slaves here when you all were running little shirt tail country stores and farming land no nigger would look at on shares" (239).

These contradictions dismantle every stance Jason takes, culminating in passages of total confusion:

> Like I say, let her lay out all day and all night with everything in town that wears pants, what do I care. I dont owe anything to anybody that has no more consideration for me, that wouldn't be a dam bit above planting that ford there and making me spend a whole afternoon and Earl taking her back there and showing her the books just because he's too dam virtuous for this world. I says you'll have one hell of a time in heaven, without anybody's business to meddle in only dont you ever let me catch you at it I says, I close my eyes to it because of your grandmother, but just you let me catch you doing it one time on this place, where my mother lives. These dam little slick haired squirts, thinking they are raising so much hell, I'll show them something about hell I says, and you too.

> I'll make him think that dam red tie is the latch string to hell, if he thinks he can run the woods with my niece. (241)

This is the Postmodern unmasking its own potential madness: unable to complete an attack or even a thought, shifting pronoun antecedents and motives with equal swiftness. Jason's indifference slides into concern, "her" drifts from Quentin to Mrs. Compson, "it" from Earl's meddling to Quentin's promiscuity, Jason's contempt for Quentin to an uncle's fiercely protective pride: "if he thinks he can run the woods with my niece"!

As much as if not more than Benjy and Quentin, Jason erects an autonomous monologue. By virtue of his mental disturbance and his parodic distortion of a literary mode, Jason creates a history of his mind and family beyond criteria of validity or value. Caddy survives in Jason's imagination as little more than another occasion for his outrage, a vague figure of sexual and financial power, deception, untrustworthiness, herself touched with madness. These qualities are either Jason's own or ones he hopes to achieve, whereas Caddy is not even the coherent fictional projection she becomes for Benjy and Quentin. Instead, like all the figures in Jason's monologue, she is little more than an abstraction, designed to focus that anger whose real source he does not know is buried beneath the contradictory symptoms of his antic behavior. "April Sixth, 1928" sustains and intensifies the sui generis quality of its predecessors. It has the unmistakable *rightness* of a brilliantly realized rendering of a mind locked within psychotic utterance, and the unmistakable *irrelevance* of a groundless discourse.

"Faulkner"

In the final paragraph of the most complete version of his 1933 Introduction, Faulkner writes that, having composed the Quentin and Jason sections in an attempt "to clarify Benjy's," he realized that he "should have to get completely out of the book," presumably in order to end it. Not that he himself had ever been "in" it, but he had written each of the three previous sections as the voice of a character who was. To be "out of the book" meant that he must adopt the voice of a nonparticipant. In the context of the modernist stream-of-consciousness mode, or the Jamesian third-person restricted mode that had preceded and to some degree made it possible, that nonparticipant could only be the omniscient narrator of the classic nineteenth-century European novel. This narrator was not only free to describe any scene, explore any mind, but also had the insight and distance to organize character and action so plausibly, and comment on both so judiciously, as to bring the entire text to some kind of persuasive meaning and valuation.

"April Eighth, 1928" concludes *The Sound and the Fury* not because it reconciles the novel's differing perspectives or offers one truer than those of the other sections, but because it is a fictional mode grounded on the assumption of coherent and significant ending. Coming in the novel where it does, however, following the radically individualistic versions of Benjy, Quentin, and Jason – no two of which agree and no one of which can be established as either accurate or inaccurate – this final view of the Compson family loses the authority inherent in its realism and its rational, trustworthy voice. It becomes the fourth mystification, the fourth episode of narrative autonomy in the novel. It lifts the depiction of "reality" to the level of original invention, overcoming its own strict referentiality, its seemingly faithful account of the truth of the world, and establishing itself as one more re-creation of the Compson story.

To be sure, we experience this re-creation with relief, given the confusion of the three previous narratives. The orderly process of the section is exemplary: a finely invoked setting – "The day dawned bleak and chill, a moving wall of gray light out of the northeast" (265); introduction and description of the remaining Compsons and their servants; gradual development of two plots revolving around Dilsey and Jason, neatly opposed in outcome and significance; and the coda of Benjy's trip to the graveyard, the place of all endings. And yet the preceding narratives have the effect of making us skeptical of this one – what do *these* Compsons and *this* rendering of their condition have to do with those we've already read? We ultimately recognize that we are once again in an invented world, albeit one deploying conventions of realism, Aristotelian narrative structure, contrasting plots, and sober, convincing interpretations of action and character.

The heart of the section is its arrangement of the dual quests of Dilsey and Jason. The plot of Dilsey's Easter observance with her family and Benjy develops as a clear enactment of the experience of wholeness: the wholeness of the community, "speaking to one another . . . beyond the need for words" (294), of the individual life redeemed in Jesus Christ, and of all history, cosmic and Compson: "I've seed de first en de last. . . . I seed de beginnin, en now I sees de endin" (297). Happening simultaneously is the plot of Jason's frantic chase after Quentin, which proves utterly fruitless, culminating in near death at the hands of a man wielding an axe. Jason's experience, the reverse of Dilsey's, is of the absence of wholeness or fulfillment. The destined location of meeting is empty: "You better go on. They aint here" (311); history does not complete itself but merely begins again its long, aimless process, "where his life must resume itself" (314).

The symmetry of the plots, the methodical movement of the whole section from beginning to end, the sudden balancing of what has been so chaotic a drama, begin to suggest still another parody, as if this new order were only the mocking imitation of a more profound one. By the end of the day disorder violently erupts. "April Eighth, 1928" tries to conclude with Benjy and Luster driving to the graveyard, but the journey aborts as Luster steers the carriage to the left of the Confederate monument instead of Benjy's accustomed right. The idiot responds to this aberration with a pure frenzy of *sound*. Earlier in the section, the narrator has absorbed Benjy's bellowing into eloquent interpretation: "It was nothing. Just sound. It might have been all time and injustice and sorrow become vocal for an instant by a conjunction of planets" (288). Now, however, interpretation fails: "There was more than astonishment in it, it was horror; shock; agony eyeless, tongueless; just sound" (320). On the brink of closure an absolute *meaninglessness* emerges, overturning narrative understanding.

Jason races into the street to turn the carriage around and send Luster and Benjy back home, away from the graveyard. Benjy instantly quiets down, and calm descends, "as cornice and façade flowed smoothly once more from left to right, post and tree, window and doorway and signboard each in its ordered place" (321). The scene is the shell of closure; the order restored has nothing to do with completed narrative, resolved tensions, intelligible history. The order is the idiot's, "signifying nothing": at once an absence of meaning at the center of omniscient narration and a fullness of meaning that refuses to measure itself by this, or any other, standard.

The Sound and the Fury pursues its extreme originality not without loss. One loss is history: the conditions of class, color, and kind that, according to much recent criticism, should constitute the language of our literary texts. As John T. Matthews has noted, Faulkner's novel is essentially "oblivious to history," registering its contexts "only in incidental details and reflections."[26] Another loss is the figure of Caddy, who is at once crucial to the novel, a dominant imagery, and absent from it, resisting definition. Readers have frequently acknowledged both omissions, occasionally regretted, sometimes even corrected them in the name of unfulfilled aesthetic, political, and moral criteria. Charges have been leveled: one omission hides various elitist, capitalist, or formalist agendas; the other – Faulkner's refusal to give Caddy a stream-of-consciousness section like those of her brothers – is a sexist silencing of the female voice.

There is no question but that *The Sound and the Fury,* unlike the Compson family, insulates itself tightly against the social forces that surround it. They are part of that world on which Faulkner had "clapped" the door, as if seeking to rid his verbal creation of everything that threatened to limit the freedom of what he might say.

As for the conception of Caddy, according to Faulkner's recollection of it, it is the novel's interior inspiration, representing nothing that is "real" or prior to the words that re-create her. Given the fact that the fictional narrators who speak those words are all male, Faulkner's pursuit of autonomy may seem to be merely another screen for sexist subjection. The context of Faulkner's career, however, as well as the novel itself, encourages us to look for other motives for the strategy of Caddy's characterization. Immediately following *The Sound and the Fury,* Faulkner gave extremely powerful and cogent voices to women – Temple Drake, Addie Bundren, and later Rosa Coldfield – suggesting that the earlier novel is powered by motives other than the need to demonstrate or practice sexual exploitation and suppression. Moreover, he repeated the essential narrative structure of that novel – of tellers surrounding a vital and yet strangely muted character – in *Absalom, Absalom!*, but in this case the character is the epitome of maleness: the powerfully virile Sutpen, whose speech is cloaked in a willfully impersonal style and who withholds, even from himself, the secret of his disaster. Like such characters as Kurtz, Lord Jim, Gatsby, Robert Cohn, Adrian Leverkuhn, and Willy Stark, all illuminated more by the tellers obsessed with them than by their own voices, Caddy Compson is a hero others must invent. The ''silence'' of Caddy in *The Sound and the Fury* crosses the lines of gender, engaging different issues: the dynamic relation of action and narration, the articulation of the wordless Other as the major action of the modern voice.[27]

The intention of *The Sound and the Fury* is to exercise, to as great a degree as possible, a will and prose shorn of context, to be the text accountable to itself. Each narrated day renders the Compson scene brilliantly within the rules of its own form of representation, even as it transgresses those rules, isolating itself into an autonomous realm of writing. The quest of each section is to become the freestanding, unverified vision of a world, determined to mean more and other than the rules of reading would always require. It is not Faulkner's greatest novel, but it is undoubtedly his first, the magnificent discovery of the difference between what had made him and what he could make: ''I said to myself, Now I can write. Now I can just write.''

NOTES

1 While this quality of resistance in writing is distinctly modern, one of its effects is to encourage us to revise our views of the past: in this case to recognize that even the most apparently doctrinaire texts, representative of periods and places characterized by rigid convention and control, can display an originality that goes beyond the rehearsal of current dogma. They speak what listeners and readers, then and now, did not know they were ready to learn.

2 F. R. Leavis, *The Great Tradition* (New York: New York University Press, 1950), p. 180.

3 Quoted in Joseph Blotner, *Faulkner: A Biography* (New York: Random House, 1974), vol. 1, p. 557.

4 Ibid., pp. 559–60.

5 William Faulkner, "An Introduction to *The Sound and the Fury,*" reprinted in David Minter, ed., *The Sound and the Fury* (New York: W. W. Norton & Company, 1987), pp. 218–24.

6 Thirteen years later Faulkner crudely dismissed the introduction: "I had forgotten what smug false sentimental windy shit it was." *Selected Letters of William Faulkner,* ed. Joseph Blotner (New York: Random House, 1977), p. 235. Philip Cohen and Doreen Fowler suggest that Faulkner's repudiation may be owing to his belief that the introduction was too self-revealing. "Faulkner's Introduction to *The Sound and the Fury,*" *American Literature* 62 (1990):272.

7 *Faulkner in the University: Class Conferences at The University of Virginia 1957–1958,* ed. Frederick L. Gwynn and Joseph L. Blotner (Charlottesville: University Press of Virginia, 1959), p. 6.

8 Ibid., p. 77.

9 Ibid., p. 1.

10 *The Sound and the Fury* is thus significantly different from *Absalom, Absalom!,* another novel laid out as a sequence of perspectives, but which provides some grounds for precisely that kind of comparative validation. By that novel's end, despite abiding contradiction and conjecture, the various narratives have merged in the final cooperative telling of Quentin and Shreve into a plausible whole, a coherent, persuasive history of filled-in fact and meaning.

11 *Faulkner in the University,* pp. 116–17.

12 Henri Bergson, *An Introduction to Metaphysics,* trans. T. E. Hulme (New York: The Liberal Arts Press, 1955), p. 22.

13 Faulkner, *The Sound and the Fury,* The Corrected Text (New York: Modern Library, 1992), p. 177. All references to the novel will be to this edition.

14 Ezra Pound, "A Retrospect," in *Literary Essays of Ezra Pound,* ed. T. S. Eliot (London: Faber and Faber Limited, 1954), p. 4.

15 Hugh Kenner, *The Pound Era* (Berkeley: University of California Press, 1971), pp. 190–1.

16 Ibid., p. 187.

17 Michael Millgate, *The Achievement of William Faulkner* (New York: Random House, 1966), p. 96.

18 Frank Kermode, *The Sense of an Ending* (New York: Oxford University Press, 1967), p. 47.

19 Frank Kermode, *Romantic Image* (London: Routledge & Kegan Paul, 1957), p. 2.

20 Ibid., p. 48.

21 Linda Hutcheon, *A Theory of Parody: The Teachings of Twentieth-Century Art Forms* (New York: Methuen, 1985), p. 35.

22 In *Faulkner in the University*, pp. 262–3, Faulkner said that Quentin never had a conversation about incest with his father: "He just said, Suppose I say this to my father, would it help me, would it clarify, would I see clearer what it is that I anguish over?"

23 "Appendix/Compson 1699–1945," *The Sound and The Fury. New, Corrected Text* (New York: Modern Library, 1992), pp. 327–348.

24 For a discussion of New South attitudes see John T. Matthews, *The Sound and the Fury: Faulkner and the Lost Cause* (Boston: Twayne Publishers, 1991), pp. 89–105.

25 For a discussion of Jason's stock market dealings see Gail Moore Morrison, *William Faulkner's "The Sound and the Fury": A Critical and Textual Study* (University of South Carolina Ph.D. Thesis, 1980), pp. 464–8.

26 Matthews, *Faulkner and the Lost Cause*, pp. 89–105.

27 For a discussion of this narrative mode see my "The Divided Protagonist: Reading as Repetition and Discovery," *Texas Studies in Language and Literature* 30 (Summer 1988): 151–78.

4

Quentin Compson: Tyrrhenian Vase or Crucible of Race?

RICHARD GODDEN

I

FAULKNER'S postpublication statements about *The Sound and the Fury* swaddle the book in maidenheads: having shut his door on publishers he "began to write about a little girl" and to "manufacture [a] sister."[1] In a further analogy, for writing he cites the old Roman "who kept at his bedside a Tyrrhenian vase which he loved and the rim of which he wore slowly away with kissing it. I had made myself a vase, but I suppose I knew all the time that I could not live forever inside of it."[2] The vase is a crackable euphemism. In *Flags in the Dust* (1927), the manuscript whose rejection caused Faulkner to close his door, Horace Benbow makes a similar vessel: having learned to blow glass in Venice, he manufactures "a small chaste shape . . . not four inches high, fragile as a silver lily and incomplete." He calls the vase Narcissa, for his sister, and is anatomically concise about the source of his skills: of Venetian glass workers, he notes, "They work in caves . . . down flights of stairs underground. You feel water seeping under your foot while you are reaching for the next step, and when you put your hand out to steady yourself against the wall, it's wet when you take it away. It feels just like blood."[3] Venice and vagina elide, even as vase and hymen cross.

The pervasiveness of the hymen is reaffirmed by Faulkner's accounts of the novel's source, which place the sexuality of small girls at the first as at the last. On several occasions he insisted that the novel "began with a mental picture"[4] of Caddy's soiled undergarment up a tree; under the tree two brothers watch the stained drawers ascend. The day of the "muddy . . . drawers" is structurally central to Faulkner; his comments suggest that the four sections "grew" from a repeated attempt to explicate that "symbolical . . . picture."[5] All of which begs the question, "Why should a sister's hymen matter quite so much?"

From a first reading of *The Sound and the Fury*, it is clear that each of the brothers has difficulties getting over his sister; her "honour" and its loss is central to them all. I have space only to outline the case: Benjy frequently shares Caddy's bed, at least until he is thirteen, and bellows at her departure or at the departure of objects associated with her (slipper, mirror-box, fire). Quentin spends a fair part of his Cambridge day trying to restore an immigrant girl to her parental house; he calls her "sister," and in memory circles back to events surrounding Caddy's protracted loss of "honour." He appears to believe that incest might serve if not to heal the hymen at least to involve the incestuous pair in a shame so great as to "isolate" them from "the loud world."[6] His preferred medium of isolation is fire borrowed, in effect, from Horace Benbow's Venetian cellars. Quentin does rhetorically what Horace did in actuality: he blows a glass maidenhead, in which "purged and purified . . . soapbubble"[7] he seeks to cleanse his sister; as brother and sister "merge" they become "a flame . . . blown cleanly out along the cool eternal dark" (176). For Jason too the question of a sister's virginity is inseparable from incest. It cannot have escaped his attention that Caddy chose to call her fatherless child Quentin. Fearing that his niece is "too much like" her mother (262), he insists on at least a semblance of respectability, but his sanctions are no match for her kimono: "I'll be damned if they dont dress like they were trying to make every man they passed on the street want to reach out and clap his hand on it"(232). The three brothers, with very different degrees of self-consciousness, "want to reach out" to their sister. Strangely, doing so involves each of them in forms of more or less recognized miscegenation.

Benjy becomes "bluegum": confronted with evidence of Caddy's loss of virginity, he immediately turns to a scene in which he is told about secondhand impregnation amongst bluegums:

> Caddy came to the door and stood there. . . . I went towards her, crying, and she shrank back against the wall and I saw her eyes and I cried louder and pulled at her dress. Her eyes ran.
>
> *Versh said, Your name Benjamin now. You know how come your name Benjamin now. They making a bluegum out of you. Mammy say in old time your granpaw changed nigger's name, and he turn preacher, and when they look at him, he bluegum too. Didn't use to be bluegum, neither. And when family woman look him in the eye in the full of the moon, chile born bluegum. And one evening, when they was about a dozen them bluegum chillen running around the place, he never come home. Possum hunters found him in the woods, et clean. And you know who et him. Them bluegum chillen did.* (69)

Late in the summer of 1909 Caddy lost her virginity. Benjy recognizes the loss – an insight which need not involve mysterious intuition. He does not stare at eyes because he has insight, but because like fire and glass the eye moves and reflects light, and at this moment Caddy's eyes are probably moving far too fast. The important point is that, upon discovering her loss of virginity, Benjy goes back almost nine years to November 1900, when his name was changed. The shift appears to have no mechanical trigger, yet there is evidence of a narrow imagination producing at least partially conscious comparisons. Caddy's sexual change is associated with Benjy's name change in an essentially cultural analogy involving two impurities: loss of virginity is likened to loss of a first or maiden name. Since Benjy had been named Maury after his mother's brother, it would seem that his sister's sexual activity has forced him to recognize linguistic duplicity. In effect, Benjy counters his disturbing insight by recalling a particular story about multiple names. A Mississippi bluegum is a black conjuror with a fatal bite. Versh's bluegum has the additional gift of magic eyes, a gift that seems to have resulted directly from a name change. Simply by looking at his congregation the bluegum preacher can make them all, even unborn children, bluegum too. As a bluegum, Benjy can claim paternity over any child his sister may have conceived in 1909. He can look into Caddy's shifty eyes and reimpregnate her in an innocent incest which involves no penetration. According to the story, Benjy is the father of Caddy's child.

The complexity of the analogy realizes a childishly simplistic purpose: Benjy wants his small sister for himself, and to that end has engaged in "plotting," inventing a temporal comparison that allows him to move from an unpleasant event in 1909 to an earlier but less troubling loss. The shift works for him because, as a bluegum, Benjy can control his sister's sexuality. My attribution of an act of consciousness to Benjy – a character most typically described as "passive and uncomprehending"[8] or "totally devoid of . . . consciousness"[9] at a pattern-making level – stems from a conviction that even those with severe learning difficulties are liable to whatever subterranean stories characterize the culture within which they pass their long childhoods.

Paul Ricoeur's account of preplotting may be useful here. He suggests in *Time and Narrative* that to experience is to be always and already emplotted. As cultural entities, he argues, we move among interwoven signs, rules, and norms which translate any of our actions into "a quasi-text"; these signs make up a cultural texture immanent with potential text, what he calls "(as yet) untold stories." So our background entangles us in the prehistory of our culture's told stories:

> This "prehistory" of the story is what binds it to a larger whole and gives it a "background." This background is made up of the "living imbrication" of every lived story with every other such story. Told stories have to "emerge" from this background. With this emergence also emerges the implicit subject. . . . Telling, following, understanding stories is simply the "continuation" of untold stories.[10]

Since, for Ricoeur, "untold stories" form the subtext from and through which subjects "emerge," acts of consciousness based on them are perhaps best spoken of as "semi-conscious," or "partially articulated," intentions. I specifically avoid the terms "unconscious" or "subconscious" because, all too often, they are associated with an absence of intention.

That Benjy should play bluegum at this precise moment suggests that even a person with a mental age of perhaps three, albeit in a thirty-three-year-old body, knows the preplots of his time. By means of a black mask Benjy, at some level, intends to get his sister back, but the end of his redemptive anecdote is problematic. "Old time" refers to slavery, during which regime a master might manifest his will by cancelling a slave's name, thereby consigning the slave to thing status by severing his or her genealogical ties at the stroke of a pen. Historians refer to this as the imposition of "natal death." Mrs. Compson, by removing her brother's name from her son (when his retardation becomes apparent) blackens her child, making him a slave to her willful preoccupation with the purity of Bascomb blood. The blackness sticks, so much so that Benjy can imagine innocent incest only from within a bluegum's black skin. It follows that sexual congress, even where only ocular, results in a guilt whose form interweaves white and black potency, and ties both to death (*"Possum hunters found him in the woods, et clean"*). The manner of that death may yet give Benjy satisfaction, since playing bluegum involves a muted revolt against the master or mother's will. Because Versh's story is an anecdote from slavery times, its hero can only be read as "uppity": the preacher takes revenge on his owner with a look implying untraceable sexual assaults on black, and perhaps white, women. Such a gaze is dangerous inside an institution so peculiar that no slave may look directly into a white eye for fear of punishment. The bluegum, after a successful career featuring *"about a dozen . . . children,"* is necessarily punished. Dilsey is the story's source (at least for Versh), and perhaps her lesson is that the bluegum dies because he is just too rebellious for a domestic servant whose life has been dedicated to sustaining a white household; but she may hand the story down because she knows that servants cannot endure masters without sustenance from a quietly subversive anecdotal tradition. Either way, the story emerges from a dense cultural web, within which white and black purposes clash and cross. Furthermore, Benjy's use of the apparently simple tale is packed with "(as yet) untold stories" about seemingly necessary relationships between virginity and incest, and incest and miscegenation. I do not mean to suggest that the network is available to Benjy, but clearly his time jump from 1909 to 1900 *is* motivated; he achieves an act of corrective incest by means of the cultural preplots to which he has been apprenticed.

Quentin's desire for incest is altogether more articulate; nonetheless it too is shadowed by intimations of miscegenation. By contemplating sex with his sister he joins the other suitors, all of whom are "blackguards" (the epithet is carefully chosen and much repeated). To elevate the presence of the word "black" within "blackguard" into a case for the interdependency of white and black male potency may look like ingenuity of the worst kind. However, Quentin cannot divorce his own sense of Caddy's sexuality from the sexuality of black women: "*Caddy? Why must you do like nigger women do in the pasture the ditches the dark woods hot hidden furious in the dark woods*" (92). Given that Caddy acts like "nigger women" in "the dark woods," it follows that those who come to her may well be "dark" or even "black," and so deserving of the term "blackguard." A similar fear of racial crossing haunts Jason's recognition that Miss Quentin is of his "flesh and blood." Both Mrs. Compson and Caddy use this phrase when urging him to support his niece (181, 209), and in each case the wording triggers, within the space of a page, metaphoric acts whereby Jason is associated with a "slave" because he works so hard (in the second instance the epithet is his own). Once used, the term sticks. The "slave" Jason is attracted to his niece, whom he likens to "a nigger wench" (189), believing that she "act[s] like [a] nigger" (181) because "it's in her blood" (232). Since he shares her blood, it is a short step from his claim that "blood always tells" (181) to the recognition that what it tells may be a tale of mixed race. He does not take this step, however, perhaps because the blood that beats in his head gives him blackouts.

"Slave" thus joins "bluegum" and "blackguard" as covert forms of blackface, by means of which the brothers achieve displaced penetration of their sister. I've traced these submerged plots through the novel's verbal latencies to suggest how, for the brothers, the sister's hymen is also a color line. In taking Caddy's virginity, no matter at what distance, each of them, metaphorically, turns "black." When the critical tradition sees these issues, it tends to psychologize them. The oedipal dragnet has been much run through Faulkner's preoccupation with incest. What generally results is some version of a primal scene in triplicate, in which brother challenges father by loving sister as surrogate for inadequate mother. Parts of the novel can be made to fit such a scenario, though not without strain, as in John T. Irwin's famously elaborate reading of Quentin's problems in terms of Freud's theories of narcissism. Since Quentin cannot accept as an object of love any "self" which does not resemble his own "self," he desires the sister, perceived as *"running out of the mirror"* (81). Such mirroring

> reveals the ultimate goal of all infantile, regressive tendencies, narcissism included: it is the attempt to return to a state in which subject and object did not yet exist, to a time before the division occurred out of which the ego sprang – in short to return to the womb, to re-enter the waters of birth.[11]

I do scant justice to Irwin's ingenuities, though it should be possible to see from my summary how certain of Quentin's obsessions (mirrors, water, castration, repetition) could be set within a Freudian frame.

The problem with this Freudian reading is what it does to the black. Irwin describes the "negro resonances in Quentin's mind" as "the dark self, the ego shadowed by the unconscious."[12] To lodge the black in a universal unconscious is to remove him from Mississippi, though any reading of Jim Crow establishes that a fearful conjunction of race and sex disturbed the Southern white imagination during what has been called the Radical era (1889–1915). Faulkner was born in 1897, Quentin in 1891, Jason two years later, and Benjy two years after that. The dates are less important than the fact that the creator and his characters grew out of a period of acute and specific racism, during which white and black sexuality became inextricable. Until the black, the virgin, and the incestuous brother are put into the Black Belt at the turn of the century, their centrality for Faulkner will not be understood. To make the case that Faulkner's plots lie in the Southern politics of race and gender (1890s–1910s), a brief history of that racial pathology is necessary.

To the conservative Southern mind the end of slavery in 1865 posed a key problem: how to position blacks in their organic place (at the bottom, as the hands of the system), without the educational benefits of the benevolent institution of slavery. "Freed," the black "child" (Sambo means "son of") could all too easily turn against the recently sustaining father (the antebellum planter as patriarch). By the mid 1880s the problem appeared to have worsened in that a generation of young blacks was coming to manhood without the "civilizing" effects of slavery. During the early 1890s fear of falling agricultural prices fostered scapegoating and the South suspected as well that Northern politicians wanted to end illegal Southern attempts to exclude blacks from the ballot. All this prepared the way for the rise of the Radical mentality, which signaled the South's "capitulation to racism"[13] between 1890 and 1915. Whereas the conservative sought to "protect" and "preserve" blacks by assigning them their proper place in the "natural order," the Radical was obsessed with the failure of that order. He feared that the angelic black child of slavery, released from the school of the peculiar institution, was becoming the demonic black adult of freedom. To the Radical, the weaponry of Jim Crowism (disenfranchisement, segregation, lynching) supplied the only means to subordinate blacks as they degenerated. One image especially focused the issue of black regression: "the black beast rapist." It can be argued that a sociosexual fantasy underpins much state legislation concerning segregation during the decades around the turn of the century. Joel Williamson makes the case that, faced with a deepening agricultural depression and the failure of political action to foster economic reform, white Southerners turned to racial action as an area in which they might at least appear to be managing their lives. He insists that Radicalism, as a system for thinking about black people, gained "absolute ascendancy"[14] in the deep South at this time. Neither Faulkner nor the Compson children would have escaped apprenticeship to its pathologies. As Neil McMillen stresses, the years between 1889 and 1915 saw the most repressive Jim Crow activity in Mississippi's history. Repression modifies the repressors as well as the repressed:

> How much would white society have to change itself and white Southerners change themselves in order to keep black people down? When they were through with the Radical era, there was hardly a facet of life in the South in which the whites had failed to respond to the black presence, and the nature of that response gave Southern white culture in the twentieth century its basic shape.[15]

White self-revision turned on the image of the black male. The plot runs as follows: during the antebellum period, Southern white males of the owning class idealized womanhood, by raising the female gentry on pedestals above the reality of interracial sex between slave women and slave owners. As the color line was crisscrossed in the quarters, so the pedestals soared at the plantation house. In the words of one Southern historian, the white woman became "the South's Palladium ... – the shield-bearing Athena gleaming whitely in the clouds, the standard of its rallying. ... She was the lily-pure maid of Astolat. ... And – she was the pitiful Mother of God."[16]

By means of her propriety, husbands, fathers, and sons whitewashed their property and its sustaining institutions. The cult of Southern womanhood raised the standard of the unbreachable hymen precisely because miscegenation breached the color line throughout the prewar South. Plainly, if the iconic figure was to withstand the iconclastic force of the realistic evidence, it needed support – support which white males found in the incest dream, institutionally reinforced by a high incidence of cousinship marriage among the plantocracy. Where the hymen stores the family "blood," protecting it from any risk of contamination through crossing, incest ensures that where crossing has occurred it shall be between like "bloods."

As the pathology whitened key whites, it blackened key blacks, producing a mythological dark couple, the woman as sexual "earth mother," and the man as "black beast rapist." Emancipation had changed the obsessional map. Freeing the slaves blocked white access to the quarters (contemporary observers agreed that miscegenation between white men and black women was much reduced). In the white mind, since the "freed" man now served the libidinous black female, his nature shifted from child ("Sambo") to satyr. By definition a satyr cannot be sated, and, unsated, he will necessarily seek the white women earlier denied him. Within this pervasive fantasy, white men, having impeded their own intimacy with white women, projected onto the black male extravagant and guilt-free versions of the sexual behavior they were condemning and denying to themselves.

These more or less "untold stories" among which Faulkner was raised provide an effective prehistory for his narrative obsession with the triumvirate virginity, incest, and miscegenation. By 1915, Radicalism was dead as a political idea, but not before its plots had entangled those raised among its extremities. Witness the sexual and narrative habits of the Compson brothers, each of whom attempts to enter his sister (or some version of her) in an incest that will shore up the integrity of his family and class, but can do so only in blackface, since white potency is inextricable from black forms. Each attempt is severely punished (cannibalism among bluegums, Quentin's castration fantasies, Jason's headaches), whereas the hymen demonstrates its punitive resilience by its trick of regeneration, at least in the white male mind (Benjy's preference for events prior to 1909, Quentin's "innocest," Jason's contradictory faith in the integrity of his "blood"). What the brothers share is not attributable to a universal psychology (Freudian or otherwise) but to an historically specific regional pathology.

To what degree is this "conscious" or "unconscious" for the author and his characters? Eric Sundquist, who has done most to illuminate these questions, has no doubt that, in *The Sound and the Fury* at least, what matters is severely repressed:

> *The Sound and the Fury* does force this central issue [the depth of racial consciousness] back into the unconscious, for there is almost nothing . . . to indicate that miscegenation or its shadowy threat is an important feature of Quentin's psychological disturbance. One might say that *The Sound and the Fury . . . contains* the repressed that returns with increasing visibility over Faulkner's career.[17]

The "unconscious," however, need not necessarily be understood as an interior space; one might argue that repeated patterns of social action (Jim Crow, for example), geared to making and sustaining particular kinds of property (that of the Southern gentry), will induce self-taught forms of forgetting.[18] If the unconscious is seen as a group-specific form of shared amnesia, its censors are historically shakable. An individual's removal from the social pressures of the group may release him or her from what that group holds to be unthinkable, enabling a return not of the "repressed" but of forgotten social complexities. In this light, Quentin's removal from Mississippi to Harvard might be crucial.

II

The critical consensus blames Quentin for his memory on the grounds that it is repetitive, deeply incoherent, and rigidly fixed.[19] Behind the unflattering portrait lie two commonplaces. The first is that for all readers June 2nd 1910 is oppressively the day of its narrator's death; the second assumes Quentin's inability to transcend the past by means of the present. Sartre's is the most famous statement of this temporal trap. Since "everything has already happened" Quentin can only and compulsively repeat a past which "takes on a sort of super-reality."[20]

I have my doubts about both assumptions. Quentin's day is filled with much more than provision for suicide: first, second, and third time readers may well find that the flatiron purchase pales in significance before the Boston Italian community, child abduction, court cases, and Caddy. The consensus might counter that the events of the busy day are directed to the terminal event, insofar as they replay obsessions centered on incest. Since incest was Quentin's way of carrying himself and his sister beyond the "loud world," it follows that the plot requires the river bed. Such a case rests on a particular version of "repetition" in which any event is a "substitute" bound by a chain of substitutions to an original object. Thus, for Irwin, Quentin's narcissism involves "an endless repetition of an infantile state."[21] It follows that New England replicates Mississippi because Quentin "makes present reality serve him as an analogue" for past realities,[22] which "he can only inadequately repeat" since they are finally deviant versions of an initial and absolute "infantile loss" (of mother or sister).[23] Although not denying that the section features high levels of analogy, as Quentin moves rapidly between Boston and Mississippi (switching from Deacon to Roskus, from Bland to Ames, from the Charles River to a Jefferson "branch"), I would nevertheless argue that analogy need not mean "repetition."

Paul Ricoeur's work on metaphor prompts a reevaluation of what Quentin might gain from the activity of temporal comparison. For Ricoeur metaphor is frequently misread as an act of substitution, so that the phrase "majestic mountain" combines a decorative and a literal term, and the reader must paraphrase in order to recover the plain truth of the mountain. Faulknerians are just as literal about Quentin's temporal analogies. Critical activity holds the present to be transparently decorative, and concentrates on cleaning it away to reveal the fixed truth of the past. Ricoeur, however, takes a tensional view of metaphor in which "impertinent predication" results from the interaction of the combined terms: the clash of the elements compared modifies their literal meanings. What results is not the obliteration of the thing referred to, but its conversion into a "split reference" which confronts receivers of the metaphor with the requirement that they make and remake reality. To revert to the mountain: both royalty and the profile of Snowdon's north face need to be understood in relation to the network of assumptions about authority, grandeur, and land ownership informing their initial conjunction (mountains are rarely held to be "proletarian"):

> [M]etaphoric meaning does not merely consist of semantic clash but of the new predicative meaning which emerges from the collapse of the literal meaning, that is, from the collapse of the meaning which obtains if we rely only on the common or usual . . . value of our words. The metaphor is not the enigma but the solution of the enigma.[24]

When Quentin calls an Italian child "sister" he creates for himself an "enigma" within which the immigrant girl's proximity (her smell for instance) and Caddy's remoteness (the odor of honeysuckle) both resist and yield to one another; their compatibility rests on incompatibilities of class, race, time, odor which will not lapse into resemblance (before passing from resemblance to "repetition"). Rather, the "sister" is a disturbing hybrid or "split reference" that creates for Quentin a conceptual need to challenge earlier versions of what sisters are and do. Where the Southern sister could (at least for a time, and at least in Quentin's head) be subjected to a "flame" that would "clean" her hymen, her Northern counterpart is dirtied with industrial fires (her face is "streaked with coal dust"[147]). My point is that, on looking at the unnamed immigrant child, he does not see Caddy, he sees the collapse of what Caddy meant to him. Whereas, in the South, the very idea of incest involves a form of cultural heroism – raising the standard of the virgin – in the North, Quentin's return to that idea is deemed child-molestation, worthy of a six dollar fine. The experience of "sister" as a "split referent" prompts a need for different terms which will allow new thoughts on the connection displayed by the comparison.

On June 2nd 1910 Quentin is prepared to recognize associative openness (perhaps directed toward a future), where before he might only have noted repetitive closure fixated on the past. The critical custom of viewing history as déjà vu and of insisting on his "fear of change"[25] consigns Quentin to a "timeless realm"[26] in which "the story does not unfold"[27] and "no newness is produced, [and] no difference can occur."[28] Yet Quentin's day has a plot, featuring events that may transform their narrator. June 2nd might be looked upon as the day when Quentin finds out so much that is new that he has to challenge the key premises of his own culture.

Deacon, the Italian girl, and the country court are central to the challenge. Quentin uses each as a surrogate through which, with increasing insight, he revises his past. On the day before his last day Quentin probably believed, as did his father before him, that the past was a fait accompli. Mr. Compson defines "was" as "the saddest word of all there is nothing else in the world" (178), thereby paralyzing time by insisting that all tenses take their form from a falsely inflexible past tense. The rubric declares that history is absolutely determinate.

On June 2nd, in thrall to "was" and prepared to die for it, Quentin learns, half by chance and half by curiosity, that the past can be reinvented. His first act on getting up is to dismantle his father's watch. Presumably he wants to escape from his father's model of time, but its inner parts prove annoyingly well made and the watch continues to tick. The events of Quentin's day revise the intellectual substance of his initial symbolic act, so that the sound of clocks takes on new meaning. By the time he returns to his room, paternal time (or, indeed, grandpaternal time), that "mausoleum of all hope" (76), inherited from his father and his father's father (or rather, from a version of Southern history), begins to sound inapplicable or "temporary." The word "temporary" punctuates the closing cadences of June 2nd and refers to a good deal more than Quentin's life. With it the son insists on the flexibility of the past and casts his father's determinate "was" as material for a dead language ("Nón fui. Sum. Fui. Non sum" [174]). To perceive the father's position as archaic requires detachment. Quentin distances himself from Mr. Compson most effectively in their final conversation. I should point out that, for me, this conversation never happened, but is instead an imagined dialogue. Asked, at the University of Virginia, "Did Quentin . . . actually have that conversation with his father about sleeping with his sister?", Faulkner replied, "He never did. . . . No, they [these words] were imaginary. He just said, Suppose I say this to my father, would it help me, would it clarify, would I see clearer what it is that I anguish over?"[29]

If the words belong to Quentin, they can be read as a considered device whereby he imitates the voice of his father, in order to expose that voice through parody. Which is not to say that Quentin is unfair. In the dialogue's initial phase, the father is given the strong lines – making a humane bid to keep the son alive by pointing out that time will change how he feels, and implying that, in any case, dead, the son can do nothing about "was." To stop here, however, would be to underplay the substance and tone of much that Quentin makes his father say. It would seem that Quentin is to grow old simply to learn that living is "stay[ing] awake . . . [to] see evil done" (176) – done by a "dark diceman" who when he is not throwing "loaded" dice is "floating" speculative "bond[s]" on a palpably fixed market (178). Heard with this emphasis, Mr. Compson becomes something of a fatalist, for whom, in the larger scheme of things, the death or life of a son can make no difference. After all, given the dicing "gods," any initiatives (be they to suicide or a revised view of the sister) are deadened. Indeed, the father concludes the conversation with an elegy to virtually everything: "was the saddest word of all there is nothing else in the world its not despair until time its not even time until it was" (178).

Quentin's Mr. Compson champions "was": he can do nothing else because, by his lights, "there is nothing else in the world." It follows that time itself is determined by a past into which present and future (tenses linked to action and anticipation) are simply subsumed ("its not even time until it was"). This is "sad," so sad that it might have been better not to have been born, since despair is not, so far as we know, a prenatal experience ("its not despair until time"). I have exaggerated a tone in order to catch what I take to be Quentin's parody of his father's habits of mind and speech (fatalistic metaphors servicing tired aphorisms). Arguably, then, at the end of his day, Quentin takes on his father's voice, to counter both its fatalistic tone and its celebration of "was" with a repeated interjection of the "temporary" ("and i temporary"). "Temporary," here, refers to much more than one son's life; it is made to embrace all the assumptions of the father, from fate to manners, and from motives for suicide to the past itself. "Temporary" also modifies an earlier version of Quentin; if the dialogue is Quentin's, then the son who speaks in celebration of incest as an escape from "the loud world" is as redundant as the father for whom any change is no change (since it is prescribed by "the gods"). "Temporary" is the key to the conversation because it puts into time both the father and the son's atemporal casts of mind.

Once history can be seen as the activity of revision (because it is "temporary"), the contours of the past are unfixed. Tick and tock cease to be "the reducto absurdum of all human experience" (76) and become a mechanical noise whose significance depends on the historian. Quentin is a historian who takes his sister as his subject.

Deacon gives him a first lesson in historical revision. Quentin seeks him because he needs a letter delivered to Shreve on June 3rd. The factotum is not in his customary haunts, however, and while looking for him Quentin reconsiders black-white relations in North and South. The sequence of his memories is revealing, being characterized by a rhythm of insight and evasion. In the post office, expecting to find Deacon, he recalls Deacon's fondness for "whatever parade came along" (82). His memory slots its subject into a black type as lover of music, good times, and display and within a page similarly fixes two "boot blacks" as "shrill and raucous" as "blackbirds." Quentin gives one a cigar and the other a nickel, and leaves them, with the recipient of the cigar "trying to sell it to the other for the nickel" (83). On this evidence Quentin is happy "to live in the fractured world of segregation,"[30] unable to learn from blacks whom he barely sees. Yet it should be noted that even here references to Deacon and to others of his color are ghosted by Quentin's self-conscious preoccupation with his own "shadow"; the black reflection cast by the white may in time take on a troubling racial tone. With Deacon still eluding him, Quentin catches a tram away from town toward the Charles River, and discovers that "the only vacant seat was beside a nigger" (86). Child of Jim Crow, Quentin speculates on verbal niceties – in the North "niggers" become "colored people" – and concludes "a nigger is not a person so much as a form of behavior; a sort of obverse reflection of the white people he lives among" (86).

"Obverse" is essential here, and should not be read loosely as a synonym for "opposite." Even in its more innocent forms, such as "counterpart" or "that which turns towards or faces the observor," the term suggests proximity rather than antithesis. The further we pursue the word, the closer Quentin perforce moves toward thought about racial interdependency; moreover, although in his statement blacks derive from whites (they reflect white behavior), the phrase "obverse reflection" in fact makes black "the front or principal surface" of white. Black primacy in the image is enhanced by the monetary meaning of "obverse," the "obverse" side of a coin being that "side of a coin bearing the principal image or inscription."[31] Earlier, at the cost of a nickel and a cigar, Quentin turned two blacks into a vaudeville routine; here, at least implicitly, he senses that blacks are the not-so-hidden face of white wealth (a truism in the Black Belt). His usage intimates that whites, in an important sense, are what blacks make.

In the context of the troubling verbal latencies of "obverse," other words from Quentin's well-known statement become unstable. Take "reflection." As Quentin debates comparative racial assumptions on a Boston tram, his mind slips from tramcar to railcar and from North to South, seeking stable racial truths. The memory of "a nigger on a mule" (86), seen from a standing train in Virginia, reassures him by providing an image of time-honored black deference. By working this strand of memory, Quentin can, in a sense, "raise the shade" that has fallen across his "reflection." In fact, he did just that: he "raised the shade," let down the railcar window and played "Christmas gift" with the Southern black (87). For the price of a quarter thrown from the train, Quentin buys back a secure image of the Negro as "childlike," given to "reliability" and "tolerance" (87). But even as Quentin reinscribes the color line (this black says "boss" *and* "young master," and is as well "static," "timeless," and serene), the tossed coin, spinning through a semantic atmosphere colored by the many meanings of "obverse," undoes his attempt. The "shade" (or shadow) on the mule may be as "timeless" as the land itself (according to Quentin he seemed "carved out of the hill" [87]), but the quarter with which Quentin buys Sambo back reintroduces a temporal note. In American coinage, the "obverse" side "always bears the date, irrespective of the device." Monetarily speaking, the "front," "principal," "obverse," and by associative extension "black" side of Quentin's quarter is neither "static" nor "timeless." As if to underline the point, Faulkner breaks into Quentin's reassuring Southern reveries: when his black seatmate on the Boston tram wants to get off, "Quentin swung [his] legs and let him pass." The unstable valencies of "obverse" inflect "pass," releasing a complex pun: light-skinned blacks may "pass" as white, a thought which, on a tram full of "mostly prosperous looking people," could encourage a Southerner to speculate as to how many "invisible" Northern blacks have already passed their masters.[32] As he is "passed" by the black, Quentin smells the river; he dismounts and contemplates his fifty-foot shadow on the water, noting that, "Niggers say a drowned man's shadow was watching for him in the water all the time" (90). If so, even in suicide Quentin will have to pass through a shadow ("shade," "reflection") cast in some part by a black story.

Some will object that I have made one or two words work much too hard. Certainly, linked latencies, no matter how numerous ("obverse," "quarter," "shade," "pass," "shadow") may remain semisecret to their user, unless the sequence of the narrative exposes what is half-hidden. Events in what I would call the "discover Deacon plot" culminate in an encounter during which the black tactfully demands that Quentin appreciate, through him, the political fullness of black experience as it transcends white definition. If we hear Deacon, blacks cease to be what white people make. Instead, we expose the surface meaning of "obverse reflection" – that all black behavior derives from white behavior – as at best partial. Deacon turns the phrase upside down, so that, for Quentin too, its covert meanings become overt. After Deacon, "black" cannot mean what a child of the Radical era would have it mean, nor can the attendant term "shadow" escape redefinition.

Deacon has for forty years played servant to Southern scholars coming to Harvard. His status as a "colorful" character stems in large part from his affection for costumes. Meeting trains from the South, he assumes an "Uncle Tom's cabin outfit," which later gives way to "a cast-off Brooks suit" (97). His use of dress is calculated, and displays a latent tendency to satire. At the station, despite the "patches" and talk of "young marster," Deacon is a servant who masters whites, and displays that mastery to them, employing a white "boy" (his is the transferred racial epithet) as a beast of burden to carry student luggage. On June 2nd Deacon's chosen guise is military, a fact which Quentin reads as a hangover from some "parade" earlier in the week. Military terms pervade their meeting (97). Deacon gives a "very superior officerish kind" of salute to a couple of freshmen, and Quentin recalls that he boasted a hatband taken from "part of Abe Lincoln's military sash." Deacon enquires as to his appearance on Decoration Day, and Quentin assures him that in the veteran's uniform he looked good enough "to make . . . general." The list could be extended, but the point has been made that Deacon is doing something very significant with military signs that Quentin fails to read. His purpose comes directly into focus with his statement of changed political allegiance: "Yes sir. I didn't turn Democrat three years ago for nothing. My son-in-law on the city; me – Yes, sir. If just turning Democrat'll make that son of a bitch go to work. . . . And me: just you stand on that corner yonder a year from two days ago, and see" (99).

Faulkner does not choose 1907 casually. In that year blacks might have given up on the Republican party as a result of the political fallout from the much publicized events in Brownsville, Texas, the previous year. In August 1906, three companies of the 25th Regiment, composed of Negroes, were involved in rioting in Brownsville: one citizen was killed, two wounded, one of them the Chief of Police. According to white townspeople, blacks "shot up the town." In November, acting on the report of a single Southern inspector, President Roosevelt dismissed the entire battalion, without honors, disqualifying them from future military or civil service. One black commentator responded in 1908:

> A considerable fraction of Negro voters in the North and West will undoubtedly desert the Republican party on account of the stubborn attitude of the President. This may result in the defeat of his party

> and of the policies which bear his personal brand. So great a matter the Brownsville fire kindled.[33]

Deacon's reference is probably to the Senate Committee report of 1907, which upheld the presidential handling of the affair, although Senator Foraker submitted a minority report denouncing the findings. Two years later, in 1909, Foraker forced an act through Congress establishing a court of enquiry to reassess the discharge. Many regarded the establishment of the court as "the most pointed and signal defeat of Roosevelt's administration."[34] Deacon's appropriation of military signs should be read within this extended context. His bearing is a declaration of political allegiance to the disgraced black soldiers of Brownsville. His politics may be confused, since a shift to the Democrats commits him to the party of black disenfranchisement, at least in the South, but his reference to a son-in-law, once unemployed and now working, would suggest that his purposes are more local and machiavellian, involving access to labor. What matters, though, is not his political astuteness but his orientation to future purposes beyond Quentin's powers of definition: when a "servant" warns the "young marster" to look for him in a parade on May 31st, 1911 (99), the specificity of time and place pales before the tone of assertion. Deacon is unlikely to be party to Democratic electoral preparations for the three-cornered fight of 1912, but his statement in standard English, addressing future political action, declares him anything but "invisible," "Sambo," or "rapist."

Unable to face what he sees, Quentin runs South: "suddenly I saw Roskus watching me from behind all his [Deacon's] whitefolks' claptrap of uniforms and politics and Harvard manner, diffident, secret, inarticulate and sad. 'You aint playing a joke on the old nigger, is you?' " (99). Quentin's anxiety is measured by the inappropriateness of his four chosen epithets. At this point, Deacon rather deserves their opposites: "immodest," "overt," "articulate," and "joyful," but he knows when he may have revealed too much; mindful of Quentin's troubled shift in attention, he reassumes a Southern Negro dialect with its attendant subordination. Whatever Deacon's idiom, Quentin cannot make him into Roskus, and his attempt to do so goes badly wrong, resulting in a displaced attribution of complex purposes to a Southern house servant. Deacon's effect can be measured by the "marster's" thoughts following his departure:

> "Yes, sir," he said. "I've had good friends."
>
> The chimes began again, the half hour. I stood in the belly of my shadow and listened to the strokes spaced and tranquil along the sunlight, among the thin, still little leaves. Spaced and peaceful and serene, with that quality of Autumn always in bells even in the month of brides. *Lying on the ground under the window bellowing* He took one look at her and knew. Out of the mouths of babes. *The street lamps* The chimes ceased. I went back to the postoffice, treading my shadow in the pavement. (100)

A certain affinity between "belly", "bells," and "bellow" embarrasses Quentin's attempt to restore terminal calm. Quentin uses the chimes to make a point his grandfather might have approved, but time's inevitable passage refuses to become "the mausoleum of all hope" (76), thereby consigning Quentin to the riverbed. It takes him to "brides" and to Benjy's insight at Caddy's wedding. On April 24th, 1910, Benjy can see into Caddy's womb. Three months later, so too can Quentin, but he attempts to revise what he sees by playing sylvan historian. He improvises a Keatsian ambience, using the fall of light between leaves to suggest a "leaf fring'd legend" ruled by "peace" and "serenity," into which a "still unravished bride" might yet be called. But, post-Deacon, the "belly" of the Keatsian urn will deliver neither "slow time" nor a regrown hymen. Quentin's position in the "belly" of his own shadow is entirely problematic. With Deacon found, politicized, and partially recognized as such, Quentin's "shadow," that is, his "obverse reflection," or black self, may yet be pregnant with claims quite at odds with those regional assumptions impacted in the emblematic virgin.

"Shadow," however, could be read as appealing exactly to received rather than revisionist truths. Given that "shadow" is proximous to questions of impregnation, it might be said to summon the "black beast rapist" from the Radical prenarratives that constitute a crucial part of the Compson apprenticeship. Once the black rapist is loose in the associative mix, "shadow" performs like "bluegum" and "blackguard": Benjy enters his sister as "bluegum," and Quentin, similarly blackened by a potent shade, uses

Keats on Caddy to modify her sexuality. In each instance a brother perversely uses the "shadow" of the black rapist to bleach out what he perceives to be a sexual stain. Mr. Compson would understand the pathology since it rises from the interlock between virginity, incest, and miscegenation prevalent in the 1890s. But it should be remembered that the "shadow" falling across this particular passage is cast by Deacon, a Northern and nonsexual figure. His shade (circa 1910) is more disturbing than any specter from the turn of the century, in that Deacon's ambitions focus on questions of politics and labor; his orientation to the future challenges the ascendancy of "was" and so potentially opens Quentin to the recognition that his father's explanations are profoundly ignorant. At the last, Quentin aborts the revised self seen through his "guide mentor and friend" (98), by treading his shadow into the pavement.

The Deacon sequence is rapidly followed by a second extended subplot of a revisionist kind, in which an Italian girl takes over as the "shadow." What distinguishes her from her predecessor is that she commits Quentin to events that will eventually force him to acknowledge the failure of his own historical reality, insofar as it derives from the cultural prenarratives concerning virginity, incest, and miscegenation. His recognition that his account of Caddy is inadequate negates the voice of his fathers and requires him to rewrite his own and their pathologies.

I run ahead of myself. Consider first the key details in the immigrant subplot in which the Italian "sister" is made bearer of Deacon's latent lesson. Quentin refers repeatedly to his sister's "black" looks. His description of her face as resembling "a cup of milk dashed with coffee" (125) involves an epithet used again only once by Faulkner, in his description of the pastor of the black church as "of a light coffee color" (293). Matthews notes the connection, arguing from it that "all foreign elements that threaten his [Quentin's] world order are in effect black"; he adds that during the day the "foreign" proliferates, implying a future during which Quentin's fixed "ideal of the South" can only further deteriorate.[35] Matthews thus deems the suicide inevitable. His account involves reading "black" in conjunction with "dirt" and linking "dirt" with Mr. Compson's version of women as "soiled." He thus establishes

Quentin as a Southern hygienist, the foolish champion of an impossible female purity, embodying an archaic regional integrity.[36] This ignores the fact that "dirt," for Quentin, is not linked to women exclusively as something which must be cleansed. The dirt on the Italian girl is not the same dirt as that which stained Natalie and Caddy; rather, it resembles "coal dust" (147). Her smell, though dirty, does not emanate from a sexual body, but from a nickel, nor does it cause Quentin to recoil (disgust belongs to the shopkeeper); instead, he is curiously attentive to the odor of the coin in the child's hand: "She extended her fist. It uncurled upon a nickle, moist and dirty, moist dirt ridged into her flesh. The coin was damp and warm. I could smell it, faintly metallic" (126). This "dirt" is not exclusively of the South, and in pursuing it Quentin encounters ethnic realities beyond his regional experience; the Boston Italian community is industrial rather than rural.

His new "sister," in her difference, and in Quentin's ignorance of it, challenges the idea of empedestaled Southern womanhood that he learned at Mr. Compson's knee. Although a misogynist, Quentin's father is first and foremost a failed idealist, whose conviction that all women are dirty (whore) serves to remind us how, once and for him, they must have been clean (virgin). So his rhetoric renovates the cult of Southern womanhood, even as it denigrates women. Some account of that rhetoric may serve to show how far an Italian guide carries Quentin beyond his culture's polarized account of the female:

> Because women so delicate so mysterious Father said. Delicate equilibrium of periodical filth between two moons balanced. Moons he said full and yellow as harvest moons her hips thighs. Outside outside of them always but. Yellow. Feet soles with walking like. Then know that some man that all those mysterious and imperious concealed. With all that inside of them shapes an outward suavity waiting for a touch to. Liquid putrefaction like drowned things floating like pale rubber flabbily filled getting the odor of honeysuckle all mixed up. (128)

The passage occurs soon after Quentin encounters the girl, and illustrates perfectly why critics have read her as a replicated Caddy who locks Quentin into "past realities."[37] Repetition appears to be the order of the day as Quentin reconsiders his "old" sister's impregnation, only to end up in a verbal maze built by the father's voice. Yet even here, before the Italian plot has evolved, there is hesitation. Three sentences are interrupted, one of which hardly starts: "Outside outside of them always but. Yellow. Feet soles with walking like." The reiteration of "outside" measures the extent of male exclusion by women. Given Quentin's virginity, the concluding "but" may correctively allude to his fear of impotence ("but one day . . ."), though the syntactical break permits the conjunction a disruptive freedom. For example, he might modify his exclusion were he to acknowledge that he spied on his sister ("but at least I saw . . ."), whereas "but" might be a synonym for "except" ("except on the occasion of incest"). In each case the hesitation, marked by the conjunction, precipitates Quentin from abstraction toward particularity. "Women" become Caddy, a transition that remains unmade because vituperation is more easily directed at a type than a person. "Yellow," in the context of the evaded tension between generic "whore" and singular sister, refers not only to the color of the harvest moon (soon to be discolored as the dried skin on the underside of feet, "soles"), but also to an implicit self-indictment: Quentin knows himself to be a coward, even as he retreats into the verbal pleasures of an idiom that no longer fits his reality. Repeating the father has its problems, however. Quentin seems unable to finish a sentence. The father may be convinced that all women walk like prostitutes, but the son can neither affirm nor deny the paternal simile. Quentin's inclination in specifying would allow him to complete the phrase, "with walking like Caddy," but his sister, refocused through the Italian girl standing at his side, is no longer a "whore" or a "virgin." Quentin stops because events on June 2nd have begun to suggest that sisters deserve a new language. With the Italian narrative still nascent, hesitation does not become impasse, and Quentin reverts to repetition. "Woman" remains a generic type – the whore full of "concealed" clients. The new and troubling sibling, however, will not go away; instead she leads her adoptive brother into actions which will force him to discard the assumptions through which he previously told Caddy's story.

The main events of the Italian subplot are the arrest and trial, prior to which Quentin's habits of mind and language tended to warrant critical unkindness. His thoughts were often "intensely claustrophobic" and "almost impenetrably private."[38] However, his day, centering on the public accusation that he has molested a child, features a clear shift in mental habit. The accuser, Julio, is "brother" to Quentin, even as the supposed victim is a second "sister," but neither repeats past events. At every point, events leading up to the trial and the trial itself form an external representation of an inner drama (the incest fable), in which Southern tragedy, relocated, comes back as a Northern farce that precipitates Quentin into historical revision. Externalization does not involve a return of the repressed, but rather requires that Quentin see key scenes in the regional fantasy of his class from below. Caddy, a somewhat soiled Palladium, becomes a dirty immigrant girl; the South's aristocratic champion, still "Galahad," albeit "half-baked" (110), reappears in the guise of an Italian worker, as worried about wages as about family; the judicial father – aptly named Squire – recomposes the Southern patriarch as a barely literate figure who writes in something resembling "coal dust" (142). The episode extends the lessons of the Deacon plot, lessons which disrupt Quentin's prenarratives and require that he recover what actually happened, released from its entanglement in the cultural prehistory of the Radical era.

My point is not that the occasion of the attempted incest "returns," but that Quentin finds it for the first time, and that as it emerges he discovers a very different brother and sister. The effect is tonally shocking. To turn from a pretrial passage (such as the account of women as "vessels of periodical filth") to the ten or so pages of stark dialogue that follow Quentin's departure from court is like turning from the densities of *Ulysses* (the "Proteus" section) to the transparencies of Hemingway at his most minimalist ("Hills Like White Elephants"). Direct report cancels "chaotic first person effusion,"[39] in large part because the first person who emerges is new to Quentin himself. The dialogue passage occurs as Quentin recovers from a fight with Gerald Bland; whether or not he is conscious, partially conscious, or unconscious during any or all of what he sees and hears is of less importance than the shock of Bland's blow to his head. The punch levels Quentin physically and intellectually, disabling those habits of perception through which he preserves a version of himself, and thereby enabling revision of that "self." "Chaos" and "effusion," rarely as prevalent as critics claim, cease as Quentin breaks the structuring myths that have grounded his account of "incest" and the "hymen," to find a different transcription of his personal obsessions.

As Quentin becomes the historian of his own and of his region's pathologies he studies the new evidence without comment. I, however, shall briefly annotate the stunned silence of his historical discovery. Quentin comes to the branch in order to call his sister a whore. Instead they talk and motives emerge: the brother is physically jealous of Dalton Ames and wishes to take his place. Impotence prevents him and provokes the substitution of a childish suicide pact for the sexual act about which he knows so little:

> I held the point of the knife at her throat
> it wont take but a second just a second then I can do mine I can do mine then
> all right can you do yours by yourself
> yes the blades long enough Benjys in bed by now
> yes it wont take but a second Ill try not to hurt
> all right
> will you close your eyes
> no like this youll have to push it harder
> touch your hand to it
> but she didnt move her eyes were wide open looking past my head at the sky
> Caddy do you remember how Dilsey fussed at you because your drawers were muddy
> dont cry
> Im not crying Caddy
> push it are you going to
> do you want me to
> yes push it
> touch your hand to it (152)

One detail is particularly revealing. Caddy, ever practical, asks if Quentin will be able to cut his own throat. Quentin's reply involves an apparent non sequitur, "yes the blades long enough Benjys in bed by now." Several elements are involved: Quentin invokes his resentment of Benjy, who slept with Caddy until he was thirteen, fears of sexual inadequacy tied up with the innuendo that all idiots are sexual giants, and a glimmer of self-recognition. The evocation of Benjy's howl has been one of Quentin's customary ways of voicing his own confusion, and that all-obscuring noise is now silent. The knife, like the howl, is a substitute. Like the howl, the knife falls away.

> dont cry poor Quentin
> but I couldnt stop she held my head against her damp hard breast I could hear her heart going firm and slow now not hammering and the water gurgling among the willows in the dark and waves of honeysuckle coming up the air my arm and shoulder were twisted under me
> what is it what are you doing
> her muscles gathered I sat up
> its my knife I dropped it
> she sat up
> what time is it
> I dont know
> she rose to her feet I fumbled along the ground
> Im going let it go
> to the house
> I could feel her standing there I could smell her damp clothes feeling her there
> its right here somewhere
> let it go you can find it tomorrow come on (152–3)

Lulled by Caddy and innocent memories, Quentin rests. The startling disjunction between the smell of honeysuckle and a cramped arm can be explained as an interval of sleep; Caddy's sudden "what time is it" may indicate an interrupted stillness. I propose that Quentin's sexual response energizes this scene, that sleep relieves him of guilt and restores his potency, and that he wakes with an erection. Caddy resists his potency, but does so in a way that balances between objection and response:

> what are you doing
> her muscles gathered

The line break could be understood conventionally, as marking a division between speech and action. However, a passage which conspicuously omits the marks whereby such divisions are negotiated – marks of punctuation and capital letters – may well foreground the spacing of the text, causing readers to make meanings from textual items (such as spaces) which are not otherwise particularly meaningful. This break could thus be read as signaling a significant pause, during which Caddy's body adjusts to changes in Quentin's body. It appears that she is not gathering herself to sit or stand, since Quentin rises first. "I sat up" is at once an embarrassed male reaction and an attempt to disguise an erection. The duplicity is contained in the knife play. Sleep rendered the symbol unnecessary, so he "dropped it" and woke to discover the absolute redundancy of the substitute. However, the symbol is easier to manage than the reality of standing straight and of his sister's gathering muscles; consequently Quentin fumbles. As they walk away Caddy seems sexually stimulated; "she walked into me . . . she walked into me again." Her arousal probably derives from an intermingling of thoughts about her lover and brother. What is clear is that Caddy (aged seventeen) departs to meet Dalton Ames in the woods and that her eighteen-year-old brother goes with her. Whether she wants him there or thereabouts depends on how "sat up" and "gathered" are disposed. She may be bumping into him because he blocks her path to the woods, or because she is flirting with him – both readings are possible and may even be simultaneous. To stress a mutual and confused arousal, as I do, is to appreciate that the physical actions and reactions of the brother and the sister constitute an erotics which both find troubling and yet exciting. Eventually, Quentin controls the contact: "we crossed the crest and went on toward the trees she walked into me she gave over a little the ditch was a black scar on the gray grass she walked into me again she looked at me and gave over" (153).

When he tries to extend his control, however, by holding her (a gesture with which he impedes her course to her lover and puts himself in the place of that lover) a tacitly sexual struggle ensues, "she was motionless hard unyielding but still" (154). Caddy's refusal to fight, "I wont fight stop youd better stop" (154), involves a stillness which says "no" ("unyielding[ly]"); her muscles ("hard") are gathered to resist. But as soon as Dalton Ames arrives, forcing Quentin unambiguously back into the role of brother, Caddy redisposes her body. Safe and sexually alert, within Ames's shadow[40] and touch, she twice calls the departing Quentin back:

"I went back she touched my shoulder leaning down her shadow the blur of her face leaning down from his high shadow I drew back look out" (155).

Again, the reader is given bodies minus all but minimal speech. Interpreting flesh has its difficulties, but does suggest just how fleshy the Quentin/Caddy liaison is. Quentin rejects a kiss whose meaning can be lodged anywhere between solace or "come-on." Whatever Caddy's motive, Quentin's extreme reaction ("look out") amounts to snatching his face and body away, a rejection that causes Caddy to request a meeting, "wait for me at the branch. . . . Ill be there soon wait for me you wait" (155). Her demand is complicated by the presence of two men to whom she has offered her face; "at the branch," Quentin will not be in the woods where Caddy intends to go with Ames, but by returning to the branch he will be returning to the scene of his and Caddy's problematic arousal. To meet the sister there might, arguably, be to fulfill a physical assignation. Whatever the case, on this summer night of 1909, Caddy loses her virginity to Ames, but not before she and her brother have prompted in one another a physically particular and emotionally difficult sensuality.

After such evidence, Quentin cannot retreat into his father's misogyny or its antithesis. To release Caddy from the trap of the "virgin/whore" is to discover his own and his sister's sexuality unmediated by his culture's "untold stories." The new evidence suggests that his sister was a confused girl, no more or less loving than many, and that he has been party to his family's misrepresentation and negation of her.

I have interpreted what is in effect the transcript of a dialogue that took place in 1909, and it is my suggestion that, toward the middle of the day on June 2nd 1910, Quentin, with scholarly perseverance, is likewise engaged. In fact he is being knocked down by Gerald Bland. The conversation at the branch, which I have read as part of Quentin's conscious attempt to revise his past, could be an uncontrolled flashback. The notions are not mutually exclusive. Thanks to the trial Quentin knows what he is doing when he hits Gerald Bland; he repeats nothing, least of all anything compulsive. Rather, he is claiming his past back for reappraisal. A punch thrown in 1910 recaptures the punch he wanted to throw at Dalton Ames in 1909 and wipes away months of misguided interpretation. The punch is not casual; Quentin strikes out at Bland whom he has previously and parodically presented as a caricature of the Southern gentleman (all "horses," "niggers," "women," and maternal approbation [91]). The fight and lengthy mopping up operations give ample time for the dialogue to be more than a flash of insight. Above all, the effect of the transcript-like conversation on Quentin's monologue argues against any claims for it as the merely unconscious record of a moment.

After the fight Quentin's tone relaxes, and as his monologue draws to its close he describes actions as though at a considered distance. It is as if, having heard the obsessive pitch to his own voice, the speaker blunts its pathological edge and is therefore able to approach areas that previously he would have avoided. This tonal transformation is clear from single phrases. On a tram back to the university, the through-draft fills "with the odor of summer and darkness except honeysuckle. Honeysuckle was the saddest odor of all, I think. I remember lots of them" (169). All morning Quentin has been nauseated by the memory of honeysuckle; by midafternoon he catalogues it among other smells and is undecided whether to grant it any special intensity. Quentin seems at several removes from himself, with the result that he is prepared to comment dispassionately on his earlier stylistic habits:

> Sometimes I could put myself to sleep saying that over and over until after the honeysuckle got all mixed up in it the whole thing came to symbolise night and unrest I seemed to be lying neither asleep nor awake looking down a long corridor of grey halflight where all stable things had become shadowy paradoxical all I had done shadow all I had felt suffered taking visible form antic and perverse mocking without relevance inherent themselves with the denial of the significance they should have affirmed thinking I was I was not who was not was not who (170)

The memory is a nightmare that has been controlled. Previously it would have been returned to as experience, now its details are reported and weighed in a discursive structure, "neither . . . nor . . . all . . . all . . . all." His tone is tired: it dismisses painful memory by underplaying the pain ("the whole thing came to symbolize"). The jumbled past tenses merely simulate an earlier style; having emptied "was" of its oppressive weight, Quentin can afford to look back on once tormenting phrases. Very soon he will consign such phrases to the precise grammatical distinctions of a dead language: "*Non fui. Sum. Fui. Non sum*" (I was not, I am, I was, I am not) are the "Peacefullest words" (174), because they possess the peace of a museum exhibit.

During the second half of June 2nd, Quentin obtains an abundance of what is effectively new information, arrived at via the dismantling of his own historical model. Time reemerges from the archetypes of a particular cultural pathology and the creative responsibilities of the historian begin. Those responsibilities are finally beyond Quentin because, with the sustaining narrative of one "was" gone, he has no meaningful context in which to place his new information. At a loss for history, not oppressed by it, he kills himself. Lord Acton recommended that the historian rise above personal social and historical situations. Carried to its extreme his suggestion reads like a suicide note: "History must be our deliverer not only from the undue influence of other times, but from the undue influence of our own, from the tyranny of the environment and the pressure of the air we breathe."[41] Since so much of the pressure on Quentin stems from the influence of prenarratives rooted in the pathologies of the 1890s, it might be pertinent to turn to Joel Williamson for some gloss on Quentin's suicide. Williamson notes that for any white child of the Radical era to break from his cultural apprenticeship may involve a form of death:

> Southern white identity . . . was intimately bound up with the Southern white image of the Negro, however unreal that image might have been. To let that image go, to see black people as people, was a precarious and exceedingly dangerous venture that exposed the individual to alienation from his natal culture and to the loss of his sense of self. It was a matter of declaring essentially, "I'm not going to be me any more."[42]

Quentin makes this declaration. His recurrent debate about "was" is reinflected by a revised cultural history, so that the past tense and the first person pronoun are set in new relation. "I was I was not who was not was not who" (170) can be phrased, "I was. I was not. Who was not? Was, not who," with the emphasis on "was" as Sartre's murderous and "unchangeable burden." Reinflected, the phrasing disperses the past along with the pronoun, "I was. I was not. Who was? Not was . . . not who." The key to both this syntactical shift and the larger narrative revision is the black. However, in the Southern mind blacks are never alone, since "Southern white culture, Southern white personality, and Southern white ideas on race, sex and moral reality are inextricably intertwined. To change one is inevitably to change the others."[43] By changing the black, Southerners risk the destruction of their sense of self. Quentin lets the black depart, particularly from the space of white sexuality, gains a sister and loses himself.

III

Williamson asks: "how [does one] take the racism, the unreality of seeing black either as child or beast, out of the Southern mind without killing the Southerner? How does one excise a functioning part of the body and yet preserve the life of the patient?"[44] Faulkner responds that one cannot. He answers, however, with only part of his voice. What Quentin narrates is an absolute reversal of Benjy's plot. Benjy wanted to keep Caddy innocent and beyond temporal change (the hymen);[45] Quentin struggles to free her, having first tried to constitute her as the type "whore," a type that the third of Faulkner's vocal inflections (called Jason) will recall and apply to all women of a sexual age.

The sections of *The Sound and the Fury* are locked in vocal contradiction. Faulkner is talking in several accents from both sides of his mouth at once. For example, Benjy and Quentin are at odds not only over sisters but over time. Benjy almost achieves the past. Quentin almost achieves a future. To reach the third section is to hear a voice that holds both temporal poles together and so is torn apart. Jason has no time for his father's times, being obsessed with cotton futures, yet he wants his father's times restored insofar as he wishes to play patriarch to a kitchen full of suppliant "niggers."

Initially, the three monologues and their confusions appear isolated from one another, but reading and rereading establishes filial conflict, at which point collisions occur between preferred words. Since "sister," used by one, refers both to a person and to that word as it is spoken by the others, "sister" becomes double and treble voiced. The brothers do not converse (Benjy cannot, Quentin has stopped, and Jason, to all intents and purposes, talks to no one but himself); rather, the reader becomes the location of a dispute. I am trying to describe not "literary ambiguity" over the meaning of a word, but a political conflict caught (care of the reader) within a word's "semantic field," a phrase usefully glossed by the linguist Vološinov:

> The word is not a tangible object but an always shifting, always changing means of social communication. It never rests with one consciousness, one voice. Its dynamism consists in movement from speaker to speaker, from one context to another, from one generation to another. Through it all, the word does not forget its path of transfer and cannot completely free itself from the power of the concrete contexts which it has entered. . . . each member of the community . . . receives the word from another voice, a word full of that other voice. The word enters his context from another context, permeated with the intentions of other speakers. His own intention finds the word already occupied.[46]

So defined, any term may be the site of historical dispute. Take the word "father." It would be fair to say that Benjy's fretful modification of time does the father's work, insofar as the invention of Caddy as an unexchangeable purity (circa 1898) protects Compson blood from all forms of social incursion. Latent in Benjy's consciousness lies the possible rehabilitation of the voice of a father whose pathology is firmly rooted in the racial assumptions of the Radical era (1889–1915). However Quentin uses it, toward the end of that era of racial rage (1910), the paternal term has passed through other contexts and into another generation. Mr. Compson may tacitly have renovated the "virgin" with all his talk of "whores," but Quentin quits the antithesis, along with its implied black, so that, by the end of his day the son no longer confesses to the father, but judges that father an archaism unfit to face changing times ("and i temporary" [177]).

To Jason, Mr. Compson always and paradoxically faced a Northern future. Jason's father is primarily "he who sold the pasture so that Quentin might go to Harvard" – a figure who turns immovable property (Compson land) into movable property (a sum of money), and who further dictates that the sum be expended to gain Northern credit in the form of status, a prestige that would promote the Compson name even as it diminished Compson substance. Jason's Mr. Compson tells a truth about the Southern economy, a truth having no place in the world according to Benjy or Quentin (prior to June 2nd 1910); for them, dependencies of blood (familial and racial) have an absolute value. For Mr. Compson, they have a variable price. This father agreed that his wife should take their daughter to the marriage market, so the second son might receive his financial inheritance. The fact that the contract between Southern property and Northern capital breaks down, voiding Jason's promised job at the heart of Northern finance (Herbert Head's bank), does not alter the point that neither land nor person lies outside the liquidities of the market. It is only apt that the father, according to Jason, should be claimed by liquid.

Seen from Jason's perspective and that of 1928, the sale of the "pasture" becomes part of a revolution in Southern land use. The pasture is turned into a golf course, leisure resource to a new mercantile class emerging from the old and persistent planter class. By 1946, in the "Compson Appendix," Jason will have become self-consciously part of the rising class, but in 1928 his social trajectory is less clear. He spends his day caught between emergent and archaic class fragments, one minute working for a merchant while playing the New York market in cotton futures, and the next insisting on the patrimonial priorities of "blood" and "name." He resolves the contradiction by preserving his own past via what the historian C. Vann Woodward calls "the cult of archaism."[47] Taking a paternal hint, he invests in "the Old South." At his mother's death in 1933, he becomes a successful cotton merchant, but not before supplying himself with the necessary capital by translating his inheritance – the Old Compson Place – into liquid assets. The father traded with a nascent leisure industry; the son deals with would-be hoteliers, "chopping up . . . [the] oncesplendid rooms into what he called apartments"[48] before selling the conversion as a boarding house. The father's golf course and the son's rehabilitated plantation are complementary sites, in which a new Southern merchant class will play and stay, doubtless admiring "the Old South" as it springs from the heads of the new South's entrepreneurs.

Jason's "father" differs from Quentin's "father" as much as both differ from the "father" of Benjy, and the three fathers don't add up to one Mr. Compson (much less the repetitive oedipal papa). Once we realize that the word "father" means so many things, with such contradictory historical and political implications, terms associated with the authority of the father ("virgin," "sister," "black"), along with their associative networks ("mirror," "water," "shadow"), will similarly split, turning the reader into the space where the vocal dispersal of the author takes place. Dispersal is exacerbated by Faulkner's choice of form. The three interior monologues represent a threefold immersion of his own voice in the vocal and cognitive peculiarities of other styles of speech. Read aesthetically, they result in a modernist tour de force. Read historically, with an eye to Paul Goodman's observation that "a style of speech is a hypothesis about how the world is,"[49] the novel comes apart, torn by the very contradictions that tear the owning class from which Faulkner comes. Either reading delivers a difficult novel, but modernist difficulty can be solved by appeals to "suspended meaning," "the writerly text," "an open ending," and other descendants of that comforting lit-crit term "ambiguity." Historical difficulty bespeaks an altogether more intractable irresolution, best characterized by returning to the tension between narrators.

Each brother does very different things with the regionally iconic sister. Benjy turns her into a pure space, aptly represented by Faulkner as a Roman vase owned by an obsessed patrician. Quentin releases her from the constraints of "type" and so unstops time. As Frank Kermode notes, "types" are "those great instruments for the defeat of temporal flux."[50] Jason sells her, or at least embezzles what she has earned from the sale of herself, and hoards the profit. None of the brothers, with the possible exception of Quentin, can debate his version of the sister, sealed as he is within his own monologue. Nor does Faulkner supply a means to measurement: there is no section dedicated to Caddy. Instead, in late interviews, Faulkner repeats Benjy's space by claiming that "she was still to me too beautiful and too moving to reduce her to telling what was going on."[51] Thus a narrative originating in a daughter's resistance to her father ("Your paw told you to stay out that tree" [39]) reaches no conclusion on father or daughter. Instead, Faulkner gives us difficult multiplicity.

The contradictions, which for me remain historical, can be relocated within Faulkner, through a notion of the author as a subject who "authors" himself by means of the story he tells. To adapt Auden: "how can I know who I am until I see what I write?" In which case, the authorial subject realized by *The Sound and the Fury* is an impossibly divided being, simultaneously the patrician (as three-year-old), the historian (as dead historian), and the investor (who cannot yet invest). Lacking authority, this author cannot reconcile himself to finishing the book as a way of coming to political terms with himself. Consequently, section four, nominally omniscient, provides no ending. I make no excuse for omitting April 8th, 1928, from my account, since I believe that it has little to do with the novel. Dilsey's resilience, Shegog's brilliant offer of redemption, Jason's concluding exercise in arbitrary power, can be and have been used to build aesthetic bridges back to what has gone before – along the lines of "the full circle" (as at the first, so at the last, Benjy plus flowers),[52] the four-part symphonic structure,[53] the tightening web of Christian allusions.[54] Some bridges have been thematic – the black community beyond the white fragments,[55] disorder followed by Dilsey's simple order of universal Easter truths,[56] redemption after the Fall. . . . Many are the ways and insights, but none offers convincing answers to the novel's key historical questions, "Who is your father?" "Who is your sister?" "Of what use is your past?" These questions are cultural, and they produce the narrative. Because Faulkner cannot answer them, *The Sound and the Fury* is difficult, unfinishable, and torn apart by contradiction.

NOTES

1 William Faulkner, "An Introduction to *The Sound and the Fury*," *Mississippi Quarterly* 26 (Summer 1973): 410–15. Reprinted in David Minter's edition of the novel (New York: Norton, 1987), p. 222.

2 Ibid., p. 224.

3 William Faulkner, *Flags in the Dust* (New York: Random House, 1973), p. 153.

4 William Faulkner, "Interview with Jean Stein," collected in Minter, ed., *The Sound and the Fury*, p. 240.

5 Ibid., p. 240. A quick flick through Faulkner's interviews and seminars will show how obsessionally he held to this story of the novel's origin. See particularly James Meriwether and Michael Millgate, eds., *Lion in the Garden: Interviews with William Faulkner, 1926–1962* (New York: Random House, 1968) and Frederick Gwynn and Joseph Blotner, eds., *Faulkner in the University: Class Conferences at the University of Virginia, 1957–1958* (New York: Random House, 1959).

6 William Faulkner, *The Sound and the Fury, New, Corrected Edition* (New York: Modern Library, 1992), p. 101. All further quotations cited in the text are taken from this standard edition.

7 Faulkner, *Flags in the Dust*, p. 180.

8 André Bleikasten, *The Most Splendid Failure: Faulkner's The Sound and the Fury* (Bloomington: Indiana University Press, 1976), p. 72.

9 Wolfgang Iser, *The Implied Reader* (Baltimore: Johns Hopkins University Press, 1974), p. 140.

10 Paul Ricoeur, *Time and Narrative: Volume 1* (Chicago: University of Chicago Press, 1984), p. 75.

11 John T. Irwin, *Doubling and Incest/Repetition and Revenge: A Speculative Reading of Faulkner* (Baltimore: Johns Hopkins University Press, 1975), p. 43.

12 Ibid, p. 37.

13 Neil R. McMillen, *Dark Journey: Black Mississippians in the Age of Jim Crow* (Champaign, Ill.: University of Illinois Press, 1989), p. 7.

14 Joel Williamson, *The Crucible of Race: Black-White Relations in the American South Since Emancipation* (New York: Oxford University Press, 1984), p. 322. Williamson's work has been formative for my argument.

15 Ibid., p. 318.

16 W. J. Cash, *The Mind of the South* (London: Thames & Hudson, 1971), p. 89.

17 Eric Sundquist, *Faulkner: The House Divided* (Baltimore: Johns Hopkins University Press, 1983), p. 26.

18 Mark Poster's account of the emergence of Oedipus as *the* bourgeois family narrative catches something of what I mean. Poster, *Critical Theory of the Family* (London: Pluto Press, 1978), p. 23. See also Se-

bastiano Timpanaro, *The Freudian Slip* (London: New Left Books, 1974), particularly chap. 11, pp. 173–212.

19 A few phrases should serve to convey the virulence of the bad press: his section has been characterized as "a chaos of broken images" (Bleikasten, *The Most Splendid Failure,* p. 136) set among "deranged musings" (John T. Matthews, *The Sound and the Fury: Faulkner and the Lost Cause* [Boston: Twayne Publishers, 1991], p. 15) and "vapid philosophizing" (Sundquist, *Faulkner,* p. 15). Few put more than "minimal faith" in what Quentin says (Donald Kartiganer, *The Fragile Thread* [Amherst: University of Massachusetts Press, 1979], p. 8) since his is the "clinical case" (Irving Howe, *William Faulkner: A Critical Study* [New York: Random House, 1952], p. 167) of someone who has clearly "gone insane" (Irwin, *Repetition and Revenge,* p. 35) – if not mad, "emotionally infantile" (Thadious Davis, *Faulkner's Negro: Art and the Southern Context* [Baton Rouge: Louisiana State University Press, 1983], p. 77) or variously guilty of "myopic intellection" (Arthur Kinney, *Faulkner's Narrative Poetics: Style As Vision* [Amherst, University of Massachusetts Press, 1978], p. 147), "willful decadence" (Kartiganer, *The Fragile Thread,* p. 13), or simply of having "no 'world' except himself" (Richard King, *A Southern Renaissance* [Oxford: Oxford University Press, 1980], p. 115).

20 Jean-Paul Sartre, "On *The Sound and the Fury:* Time in the Work of Faulkner," collected in Minter, ed., *The Sound and the Fury,* p. 255.

21 Irwin, *Repetition and Revenge,* p. 38.

22 Kinney, *Faulkner's Narrative Poetics,* p. 147.

23 King, *A Southern Renaissance,* p. 115.

24 Paul Ricoeur, "The Metaphoric Process as Cognition, Imagination and Feeling," collected in Sheldon Sacks, ed., *On Metaphor* (London: University of Chicago Press, 1979), p. 144. See also Ricoeur, *The Rule of Metaphor* (London: Routledge and Kegan Paul, 1978), particularly study 1, pp. 9–43.

25 Olga Vickery, "*The Sound and the Fury:* A Study in Perspective," *PMLA* 64 (Dec. 1954): 1017–37, collected in Minter, ed., *The Sound and the Fury,* p. 301.

26 Myra Jehlen, *Class and Character in Faulkner's South* (New York: Columbia University Press, 1976), p. 43.

27 Sartre, "On *The Sound and the Fury,*" p. 253.

28 Bleikasten, *The Most Splendid Failure,* p. 131.

29 Gwynn and Blotner, eds., *Faulkner in the University,* pp. 262–3.

30 Davis, *Faulkner's Negro,* pp. 92–3.

31 Definitions drawn from *The Random House Dictionary of the English*

Language (Unabridged) (New York: Random House, 1966), and from *Webster's Third New International Dictionary* (Springfield, Mass.: Merriam-Webster, 1961).

32 Matthews, *The Sound and the Fury: Faulkner and the Lost Cause,* p. 102. See also his important essay, "The Rhetoric of Containment in Faulkner," collected in Lothar Hönnighausen, ed., *Faulkner's Discourse* (Tübingen: Max Niemeyer Verlag, 1989), pp. 55–67.

33 Kelly Miller, "Roosevelt and the Negro," collected in his *Radicals and Conservatives* (New York: Schocken Books, 1968), p. 319.

34 John Hope Franklin, *From Slavery to Freedom* (New York: Alfred A. Knopf, 1980), p. 316.

35 Matthews, *The Sound and the Fury: Faulkner and the Lost Cause,* p. 103.

36 "Quentin has a very self-conscious sense of how life should be, which derives most of its force from notions of gentility and *noblesse oblige* traditionally attached, in the South, to the plantation aristocracy.... [he] has constructed [an] idealized version of things . . . that has himself as a gentleman at its centre, and the purity of white womanhood (and of one white woman in particular) as its emblem and apotheosis." Richard Gray, *Writing the South: Ideas of an American Region* (Cambridge: Cambridge University Press, 1986), p. 212.

37 Kinney, *Faulkner's Narrative Poetics,* p. 147.

38 Gray, *Writing the South,* p. 211.

39 Sundquist, *Faulkner: The House Divided,* p. 12.

40 I would stress that the branch transcript is for the most part without shadows and their attendant racial pathology. Incest, and its founding term "virginity," do not prompt the co-presence of miscegenation. Gone are the "bluegums," the "blackguards," and the "blackouts." Where "shadow" does occur (four times in the space of less than a page) the term is focused on Dalton Ames, and is used to mythologize a rival's potency. Indeed, Quentin self-consciously withdraws from the shade, "the blur of her face leaning down from his high shadow I drew back" (94).

41 Lord Acton, quoted by E. H. Carr in his *What Is History?* (Harmondsworth: Penguin, 1967), p. 44.

42 Williamson, *The Crucible of Race,* p. 499.

43 Ibid, p. 498.

44 Ibid, p. 499.

45 What I have said about Benjy credits him with a temporal paradigm and a consciousness capable of organizing his experience around that paradigm. This is at odds with prevalent critical accounts which either

sentimentalize him as a moral touchstone (a vessel of the heart uncontaminated by intellect) or mechanize him, reducing him to a camera with a tape recorder attached. Kinney is exceptional in recognizing the "assimilative" force of "Benjy's narrative consciousness" (*Faulkner's Narrative Poetics,* pp. 141–2). See also Godden, "William Faulkner and Benjy Compson: The Voices that Keep Silence," *Essays in Poetics,* Vol. 4, No. 1 (1979), pp. 1–19.

46 V. N. Vološinov, *Marxism and the Philosophy of Language* (New York: Seminar Press, 1973), p. 199.

47 C. Vann Woodward, *Origins of the New South* (Baton Rouge: Louisiana State University Press, 1971), p. 154.

48 William Faulkner, "Appendix/Compson: 1699–1945," *The Sound and the Fury. New, Corrected Text,* p. 343.

49 Paul Goodman, *Speaking and Language* (New York: Random House, 1971), p. 171.

50 Frank Kermode, *The Classic* (London: Faber, 1975), p. 62.

51 Gwynn and Blotner, eds., *Faulkner in the University,* p. 1.

52 Bleikasten, *The Most Splendid Failure,* p. 184.

53 Maurice Coindreau, "Preface to *The Sound and the Fury,*" *Mississippi Quarterly* 19 (Summer, 1966): 107–15.

54 Many readings make the appeal; see particularly Carvel Collins, "Faulkner and Mississippi," *University of Mississippi Studies in English* 15 (1978): 139–59.

55 James Snead, *Figures of Division* (New York: Methuen, 1986), pp. 35–9.

56 Vickery, "*The Sound and the Fury:* A Study in Perspective," 308–11.

5

Trying Not to Say: A Primer on the Language of *The Sound and the Fury*

NOEL POLK

FLOWER spaces that curl, a fence, a search, a table, a movable flag, and a pasture in which people are "hitting," all without any apparent relationship to one another, dot the visual landscape of the opening lines of *The Sound and the Fury*.[1] And, as if the first paragraph didn't throw enough problems at the reader, the opening words of the second paragraph, the novel's first spoken words – "Here, caddie." – are relayed to us by the same narrator who has thrown us asea in the first paragraph, who transmits them without identifying their source, and who misunderstands them. They contain an aural pun, a homophone, and are related, though we don't yet know how, to the narrator's inexplicable reaction. Careful readers will pretty quickly figure out that the narrator is looking through the fence at a golf course, and a really alert reader might, even this early, suspect that the course was once a pasture, and so be able to negotiate an uneasy narrative collaboration with the opening paragraph; but these two "spoken" words, which both are and are not what they seem to be, throw us back into uncertainty.

For the speaker, the word "caddie" has a specific, unproblematic referent, and he or she assumes that the person holding the golf clubs will know what he or she means; readers, who see the words' written representations rather than hear their sounds, perforce share this assumption and adduce from it that the speaker is probably a golfer (the speaker could be a supervisor or even somebody on the narrator's side of the fence who needs the caddie's attention for some reason). Our narrator, to the contrary, does not read the words but hears the sounds that stand for the words, and what he – or she: we don't yet know the gender – hears is "Caddy" or, more precisely, some form of the sounds a phoneticist would transcribe as *[kædi]* or, probably closer to Faulkner's pronunciation, *[kædI]*. These sounds have a single referent for the narrator, a referent quite different from the golfer's and, at this point in the novel, quite different from the reader's.

The narrator's response to this lingual, aural, and visual crux – "Here, caddie." – is curious indeed. He does not describe his response or even identify it as a response; we understand that he is thinking or doing *something* only because he quotes a character named Luster. We thus have access to the narrator's response, whatever it is, only through a triangulation off the secondary reaction of Luster, who also does not describe it but merely comments about it in a way that indicates it is some kind of sound, vocal but not necessarily verbal: "Listen at you, now. . . . going on that way" (3). The narrator's vocal "response," then, which we later learn can range from simple whimpering and slobbering to horrific bellowing, is at very least an unsettling narrative non sequitur. At most it is a monstrous violation of the fictional tradition that identifies a "narrator," especially a first person narrator, with a point of view and demands that narrators be self-conscious enough to describe what is happening to others and to themselves, to let us know that something is happening, to give us reason to believe that they have some communicable sense of the possible relationships among events and of the events' significance, even if that sense is only fragmentary and speculative, and even if they don't, won't, or can't tell us all they know. The tradition assumes a direct, complex, relationship between the language narrators use and the events they narrate or objects they describe; it has thus allowed us to assume that narrators *have* a point of view and a reason for narrating, and that they are necessarily engaged in some conscious control of the materials they narrate.

Readers looking for such narratorial control in the opening paragraphs of *The Sound and the Fury* will not find it. Nothing that happens, nothing seen, heard, or felt is causally related to anything else: golfers do not hit balls, they just "hit"; Luster doesn't throw a rock at the bird on the flag, he just "throws"; the narrator doesn't even register his own reaction to stimuli as a reaction. Since he sees no relationship between one thing and another, he can't even grasp his own relationship to the world. He assumes himself to be the unmoved and unmoving center of the world: falling, he feels the ground come up to hit him; whirling, he sees stationary cows run uphill (20–1). Thus he experiences the world as a jumbled and unstable convergence of unconnected phenomena and to the extent that we share his disorientation and confusion, Benjy may be taken as a sort of surrogate "reader" in these opening pages, though our disorientation and confusion become more acute than his as Faulkner broadens the range of unattached signifiers in the next few pages. Benjy doesn't have any trouble understanding which of the two "Quentins" or "Jasons" is meant, but we do, until we have enough information from other parts of the novel to allow us to figure it out.

Benjy can register simultaneity, but not temporal or spatial relationships, except of the most primitive kind. When the golfers "go away" from him, for example, he sees them "hitting little" (3). John T. Matthews observes that "little" in this phrase is an adjective that has "usurped" an adverb's place and in doing so has "drain[ed] the verb of its energy and slow[ed] it into a picture."[2] I suggest it is even more to the point to think of "little" as the predicate adjective in a version of Benjy's sentence that we might reconstruct as "Then they were little, hitting," or, more completely, "Then they seemed small, all the way across the golf course, and were hitting the ball." The golfers are not necessarily putting, which many readers have taken the phrase to mean; rather, Benjy is noting the golfers' size at their distance across the pasture relative to their size when they were closer to his fence. The words thus represent the perspective of a primitive painting, in which all images appear on a flat vertical plane that has no calculus for spatial relativity. Faulkner will specifically evoke this plane in the fourth part of the novel when he describes Dilsey's church as belonging to a scene "as flat and without perspective as a painted cardboard set upon the ultimate edge of the flat earth" (292).

Benjy exists as much outside of space as outside of time. He has no language, since language can exist only at the juncture of time and space: signifiers and signifieds find each other and create meaning only at pinpointed cruxes where word sound and referent become one by mutual agreement between sender and receiver. The opening section of *The Sound and the Fury* is awash in signifiers that are attached to no particular signifieds – or seem that way, until readers get enough information from other sources to be able to attach them meaningfully. Nearly everything we presume to know from Benjy's "narration" we must reconstruct from various triangulations between what Benjy hears and sees and feels and what he reports somebody else saying or doing. The author's place in this triangular structure is deliberately complex and problematic; his concern is not so much to narrate as to represent narration or, more specifically in the Benjy section, not to narrate but to represent, to re-present the world in ways that bypass the filters of language that modify our relationship to experience. But Faulkner first has to force us to reconsider the relationship between words and the things they pretend to name. The opening pages of *The Sound and the Fury* rip signifiers from signifieds radically and dramatically, and those first "spoken words" – written representations of vocal sounds which readers encounter as silent marks on a sheet of paper – are an important clue to what Faulkner is about in this most linguistically radical of all his novels: to explore the relationship between language and experience, between language and reality, and between language and its oral and written representation. This essay is primarily concerned with the last of these.

Benjy's response to the golfer's command is not a matter of misunderstanding the sounds the golfer makes; he does not misunderstand what he hears, though he does misunderstand what the golfer says. Inscribing the scene on paper, Faulkner had to decide how to represent that sound, *[kædI]*, visually, whether to use some form of standard or dialectical written English, which is both more and less referentially precise than the sound itself. He chose a deliberate misdirection, a miscommunication, or perhaps *dys*communication, with his reader *and* with his narrator. If he had written that the golfer says "Here, Caddy." he would have misrepresented the unambiguous intent of the golfer's oral communication, though he would have more accurately represented the meaning that Benjy ascribes to those phonemes. He chose, then, to misrepresent what Benjy, our "narrator," hears rather than what the golfer says.

One of the great achievements of *The Sound and the Fury* is that in a novel which most critics now agree is centrally concerned with language, in a novel three of whose sections are "monologues" that make some gesture toward orality, Faulkner turns the clumsy mechanics of the representation of that language on paper, what Stephen Ross calls "the visual discourse of our reading,"[3] into a highly expressive part of the language itself. At one very simple level, reading, especially the reading of dialogue, involves translating one sense impression into another: the author translates the aural into the visual, readers translate the visual back into the aural – or should, if they want to understand *The Sound and the Fury.* For just as he plays with Benjy's hearing of the phonemes *[kædI],* so does Faulkner play with the way we read, with the mechanical signs of punctuation and spelling that harness and control, that give rhythm and shape and weight and expressive meaning to, the silent words that appear on the paper. Throughout the novel he uses an inventive array of visual devices in punctuation – or the lack of it – and spelling and grammar to help us focus on the way we comprehend language, written and oral.

Each brother, Judith Lockyer argues, "reveals an aspect of the power in language. That power is born out of the relation of language to consciousness."[4] I would suggest more: Faulkner uses the mechanics of the English language – grammar, syntax, punctuation, spelling – as a direct objective correlative to the states of each of the narrators' minds. The mechanical conventions of the writing, then, sometimes work *against the words themselves,* so that they reveal things other than what the characters are saying; they work, in fact, to reveal things that the narrators are incapable of saying or are specifically trying to keep from saying, things that have caused them pain and shame. Words are, for Quentin and Jason at any rate, lids they use to seal that pain in the unconscious, though it constantly insist on verbalizing itself. We have access to their pain largely through what they *don't* say, and also through the visual forms of the language in which Faulkner has inscribed their thoughts and feelings on paper. Benjy's section prepares us powerfully for the much more complex linguistic situations in the next three sections.

I. Benjy

Faulkner captures the disrelatedness of Benjy's various perceptions by drastically simplifying the referentiality and the mechanics of his language. Irena Kałuż describes Faulkner's prose in this section very usefully:

> Benjy's nouns do not admit synonyms, are never modified and are rarely replaced by pronouns. Thus Benjy's beloved sister is always "Caddy", whether she is seven or nineteen years old; she is rarely referred to as *she*, and never as *sister*, *girl*, etc. The same happens with the names of the other members of the Compson "family", white and black, each of them being usually designated by only one name, such as Quentin, Luster, Father, Mother. Only twice in Section One does Benjy meet strange people: a group of Negro washerwomen . . . and two girls in the street. . . . Their conversations are recorded as heard by him, but are not accompanied by the routine formula "he/she said" or "(a name) said." Benjy does not know their names and to give them identity in terms of description is beyond him. The same is in a way true about names of things. For instance in
>
> > She broke the top of the water and held a piece of it against my face,
>
> more is involved than lexical poverty or ornamental metaphor. . . . By attaching to what really is a piece of ice the name of "a piece of water" the rigid inflexibility of Benjy's world asserts itself: he used to know this thing as "water" so "water" it remains for him."[5]

Many have noted that Benjy is "pre-lingual," that he "could never really narrate his section"[6] because he has no language. But he is in fact *non*lingual: the language of the Benjy section is *Faulkner's* language. Properly speaking, Benjy is not a narrator at all, but the "very negation of narrative," as André Bleikasten has suggested;[7] he is merely a filter, and not necessarily an ordering one, for the thousands of sense impressions he processes every day, which may remain just as confusing for him as they do for readers. Benjy exists in a direct relationship to things. His world contains a multitude of signifieds, but only a severely limited number of signifiers. Even the signifiers that Benjy does attach to certain referents – Caddy, Mother, Luster – are for the most part vocal equivalents that he associates with those signifieds, although that is ultimately what spoken words are. Nevertheless, there are few verbal filters between him and the world he experiences, and it is useful to keep in mind that Benjy does not use words; he does not *tell* us things, but experiences the world directly. Benjy's "narration" is almost completely visual, cinematic, and what rolls through his mind is not "memory," although it is convenient to call it that in this essay, but rather more nearly different reels, perhaps, from a movie of his life. We can best "read" Benjy if we do not take it that he actually says, or thinks, "between the curling flower spaces, I could see them hitting" (3), but rather that the words are Faulkner's visual representation of what Benjy sees, at the precise moment of seeing; he does not actually verbalize that the golfers are "going away," he just registers visually that they are doing so. Moreover, since Benjy is not capable of describing and so of differentiating one sensation from any other, we can account for the profusion of synesthesia in his section; he does not actually *say* that "The sun was cold and bright" or that he could "smell the bright cold" (6), but rather reflects the physical sensations of what we would call "cold" and "bright" and the visual sensation of "sun" as registering on him simultaneously.

The written language of the Benjy section stands as a direct objective correlative to Benjy's physical and visual sensations and may best be taken as the direct linguistic counterpart to a primitive painter's technique. As many others have pointed out, for example, the section consists almost entirely of simple sentences, sometimes strung together with coordinate conjunctions. Just as his mind allows no distinctions among his sensations that would put them in some kind of ordered relationship, so does his language refuse what Kałuża calls a "syntactical hierarchy."[8] There are almost no subordinate clauses in Benjy's section, and so almost no subordination, no adjectival or adverbial modifications, that would demonstrate hierarchical or causal or value relationships among the sensations Benjy registers. Mechanically, there are not even variations in end punctuation that would register differentiation in the way he processes sensations, much less how they affect him or even if they affect him at all. Faulkner uses only periods for sentence endings, even in quoted matter, not question marks, exclamation marks, dashes, colons, or commas,[9] a brilliant device that flattens all emotion out of Benjy's "quotations," forces grammatical equality on them, and even detaches them from their sources. Just as all his statements are grammatically equal, so are the ideas, the sensations they convey. That Benjy's bellowing is grammatically the equal of the bright shapes that accompany him to sleep may suggest that if there is an emotional hierarchy at whose top is loss – of Caddy particularly, but also of everything else – it nevertheless remains true that all sensations seem to register equally, and unrelatedly, on him. We can gauge the relative strength or complexity of his reactions – indeed, determine whether he is having a reaction – only by listening to how other characters react to, verbalize, his vocalizations as bellowing or whimpering. Of his own vocalizations, whether bellowing or whimpering, Benjy can only note that he "stopped" or "started," not, usually, what he is doing; later in the section he does several times note that he is crying, but readers cannot tell whether he means to indicate simple weeping, or something more aggressive, like bellowing. The loss of Caddy and reminders of that loss register more strongly on him than other sensations, but he registers them at an emotional level to which he does not have verbal access. Obviously he has strong *feelings,* but because he has no access to normal language conventions, he may be as estranged from them as he is from his testicles. The problematic relationship between language and sexual urges will become clear in Quentin's and Jason's monologues.

April 7, 1928, begins with Benjy and Luster at the fence which separates Benjy from the pasture, and follows them as they work their way toward the house at the end of the day, back from the sight of one of the important things he has lost – his pasture, and we cannot help noting (Faulkner's little joke) that Luster, too, is looking for "balls" – to the dark and forbidding Compson house, the locus of all loss in the novel. On their way they pass various places on the Compson grounds that trigger Benjy's "memory" of events that have taken place there. He does not experience these excursions into the past as memory, because he cannot distinguish past from present. He is rather transported in his mind to scenes of his childhood, most centering on trauma and transition, loss;

all of them together give us a partial history of the Compson family. His transportation is triggered, as in Proust, by the repetition of something familiar and significant. Thus when he gets caught, yet again, on the fence that he and Luster crawl through, he remembers a similar incident when Caddy "uncaught" him (4) from the same fence when they were delivering Uncle Maury's note to Mrs. Patterson.

Faulkner signals these movements through time by using italics, but the italic passages are more than just visual signals of time shifts. They represent images buried in Benjy's unconscious which work their way into the front of his conscious life, his narrative present, elbowing April 7 out of the way, until it, too, pushes its way back into what registers, also in italics. Thus *"Caddy uncaught me"* (4) opens a passage of two italicized paragraphs that recount the episode in which they deliver Uncle Maury's letter to Mrs. Patterson. It begins as a dim and fuzzy italic shape in his memory as he gets caught on the fence, then emerges completely into focus as a full-blown scenario in the next paragraphs, in roman type, which throughout his section represents what is currently at the front of his mind. The roman passage does not continue the narrative begun in italics, however, but reverts to the time a few minutes earlier that far off day, two days before Christmas of an unspecified year, when Uncle Maury and Mother permit Versh to dress Benjy warmly and take him out to the gate to meet Caddy as she comes home from school. When Caddy brings him inside, Uncle Maury calls her aside, obviously to give her the letter to Mrs. Patterson, although Benjy does not know that (5–9), and readers, again, must figure this out eventually from other evidence. The narrative seems to be working its way forward to his getting caught on the treacherous fence that triggered the whole memory. But remembering Caddy's warmth, how she smelled like trees (6), makes Benjy moan on April 7, and he reports Luster's response, *"What are you moaning about"* (6) in italics. Faulkner thus uses the italics in this instance to remind us of Benjy's narrative present. They represent the intrusion of the present into Benjy's past, and suggest just how freely dissociated from time and space Benjy is.

After the brief italicized interruption, Benjy continues the narrative of Caddy's arrangements with Mother to take him with her on her errand. Two italic interruptions – *"Hold still now"* and *"Now stomp"* (8) – float freely in Benjy's head as he is mindful of numerous other times Versh has helped him dress, but the narrative of that December 23rd continues to move forward until Benjy registers Caddy's assurances: "Haven't you got your Caddy." He is again confronted with her absence, and he begins to howl. Luster again responds: *"Cant you shut up that moaning and slobbering, Luster said. Aint you shamed of yourself, making all this racket. We passed the carriage house, where the carriage was. It had a new wheel"* (9). By this time on April 7, Luster lets us know, they have come to the carriage house and the sight of the "new wheel" trips Benjy's recollection of the time when T. P. drove him and his mother to the cemetery, and he follows that memory until they meet Jason and try, unsuccessfully, to get him to go to the cemetery with them (9–12). The bright shapes of the town remind him of the bright fast smooth shapes of his sleeping, which he associates with Caddy, which in turn causes him to cry again, and Luster to respond again, and he reverts to his original memory. He finally completes the December 23rd narrative (12–14), which ends, not with a successful delivery of Uncle Maury's note, but, traumatically, with a related occasion, layered into the December 23rd foray, when he delivered the note by himself, causing Mrs. Patterson to be angry at him and Mr. Patterson to chase him with a hoe (13–14) – a metaphorical scythe prefiguring his castration.

Faulkner thus achieves the effect of cinematic montage. He juxtaposes telling episodes in the Compson family history by alternating between episodes – Benjy's encounter with Caddy and Charlie in the swing, for example, is intertwined associatively with a similar, later, encounter with Miss Quentin and her boyfriend in the same swing; Caddy's wedding and Damuddy's funeral are intimately intertwined in this same way. Through these juxtapositions, these comparisons and contrasts of scenes, Faulkner creates meanings, hierarchies of emotions and significances, that Benjy cannot. At the top of the hierarchy is his loss of Caddy, which registers most powerfully and most constantly – on himself and on everybody else.

II. Quentin

Benjy tries to say and can't; his brothers try *not* to say, and can't avoid it. Benjy's "memory" works in large discrete units. Scenes spring to life through triggers – a sound or an object – that can usually be located in the sentence or two immediately preceding the time shift (see Godden's essay in this collection for an interesting and significant exception). These scenes become interchangeable with each other as they suit Faulkner's needs, for example, to juxtapose Caddy's wedding with Damuddy's funeral and the ways in which the events are related in Benjy's mind, in Compson family history, and in the novel's movement toward significance. But Benjy is a passive receptor of these cinematic reels; he seems to have little control over what passes through his mind, and it may not be unreasonable to think that the linear separation of the scenes on the page is a function of the limitations of writing, and that Benjy experiences all of them as a simultaneous and inextricable welter of images, just as he does the "bright cold," not as separate phenomena. For Benjy all these scenes are undifferentiated, equivalent. As on a primitive painter's canvas, they appear in size and proportion as he originally experienced them, neither increased nor diminished nor distorted by perspectives of time or position.

Quentin's relationship with his past is quite different. Episodes, telling moments from the past do indeed exist in degrees of intensity, of psychic pain, which his consciousness has dwelt upon, worked through and over, in ways that continue to torture him. Like Benjy's, all of Quentin's past tries to crowd in on him at once, every painful episode tries simultaneously to elbow its way past all the others into consciousness. But whereas Benjy's memory is flat and two-dimensional, like his prose, Quentin's is like a large fluid-filled balloon that he is trying to flatten out, to control; every time he steps on one spot, on one painful memory, the balloon erupts upward and outward at another point, constantly reshaping itself to its own pernicious energy.

Quentin cannot control the chaos of his amoebalike memory and he finally succumbs to it. The protective walls he builds with his formal eloquence are constantly breached by visual intrusions from his past, italicized fragments of phrases and images that emerge briefly, even flickeringly, in no apparent order or relation, through the barriers of his language before he is able to stamp them down again, in his futile effort to keep them from full verbalization. His memories evolve out of scenes of trauma, all centered in his loss of Caddy: her wedding, his conversation with Herbert Head, the husband his parents trapped for her; her love affair with Dalton Ames and his (Quentin's) humiliating inability to defend her honor; and his long conversation with his father, whether real or imagined, whether a single conversation or an amalgam of several similar ones, about the meaning – or the meaninglessness – of life. The substance of his monologue is his effort to sort out, analyze, and come to terms with those scenes of pain that he *can* handle, and to evade, to repress, those he cannot. He is trying to shape his memory into an acceptable version of his life that will both explain his present misery and justify his decision to commit suicide, and language is the only tool he has to effect the shape he wants.

Faulkner records Quentin's efforts to control his thoughts in several ways; as in the Benjy section, none is more striking than the mechanical representation of his syntax, grammar, and punctuation, which, also like Benjy's, become objectively correlative to the state of Quentin's mind. The more in control he is, the more intricate and sophisticated the structure of his sentences, the cohesion of his paragraphs; the less lucid his mind, the less formal or "normal" the representation of his language on paper becomes. One can trace Quentin's psychic disintegration, his movements into and out of lucidity, in the degree of normality of his language's representation, from the intricately structured sentences of some passages, to the almost complete disintegration of traditional language representation in others, especially in two scenes close to the end of his section that abandon punctuation and paragraph indentation, and in the penultimate paragraph of his section in which he finally yields up the capital "I," the orthographical symbol of the fragile ego he has managed to cling to, to the lower case "i," which represents graphemically his disintegrated self. Each of these three scenes springs into consciousness at moments when his psychic censors are completely relaxed. The crucial one, significantly, the one recounting Caddy's love affair with Dalton Ames and his ineffectual efforts to stop it, occurs when Quentin is literally unconscious, or at least floating in some twilight zone between consciousness and unconsciousness, having been knocked out by Gerald Bland. Language's grammatical formality is for Quentin a conscious way to keep away from those things he does not want to think, those things he does not want to say. The mechanics of the written representation of language become Faulkner's device to let readers know how successful Quentin is: the most painful scenes are the farthest removed from representational normalcy.[10]

Throughout the section there are passages in which he is, or seems to be, in complete control. In such passages Quentin is very much like Hemingway's Nick Adams as he minutely and preciously puts into words every possible sensation, every possible observation of the moment, trying to control the various signs that would remind him of something painful back home. At his best he is capable of being ironic and self-reflexive, quite witty and inventive in his wordplay, as in this tortuously involuted mélange of negations and tenses, in which he mordantly contemplates his own demise:

> Hats not unbleached and not hats. In three years I can not wear a hat. I could not. Was. Will there be hats then since I was not and not Harvard then. Where the best of thought Father said clings like dead ivy vines upon old dead brick. Not Harvard then. Not to me, anyway. Again. Sadder than was. Again. Saddest of all. Again. (95)

Thanks to his sister's new husband, he is preternaturally conscious of heads, and so of the hats which Harvard underclassmen must wear. He is keenly aware of the different states of the heads and hats he sees from his high vantage in the train window: some heads are topped by brand new, "not unbleached," hats – that will "unbleach" as they are worn for three years – and others, usually those of seniors, not wearing hats at all. This observation leads him to think of his own senior year, three years from now, when he won't have to wear a hat if he chooses not to: "I can *not*." But his senior year is highly problematic for him, knowing what he knows, so he immediately jumps to the subjunctive: "or, rather, I *could* choose not to wear a hat if I were going to be here.

But I won't be here; in three years I will have been *was* for three years and hats won't matter to me, nor will Harvard. Will hats or, indeed, even Harvard itself exist if I am not here to affirm that they do? They won't exist at all as far as I'm concerned, at any rate." The final sentences, fragments, of the paragraph revert to his continual dialogue with his father over whether death – being *was* – is a sadder condition than continuing to live in eternal recurrence – *again* (178) – and having to experience pain and loss over and over.

Quentin is capable of poetic analogies, similes, and metaphors, of complicated but perfectly balanced parallel structures and modifications:

> I quit moving around and went to the window and drew the curtains aside and watched them running for chapel, the same ones fighting the same heaving coat-sleeves, the same books and flapping collars flushing past like debris on a flood, and Spoade. (78)

Quentin's sentence works to contain, to control, all the moiling activity of the Harvard yard below his window, the running and fighting and heaving and flapping and flushing, within its intricately parallel compound-complex structures. Spoade intrudes upon his ordering vision and so upon the sentence's structure. Strictly speaking, "Spoade" is the second element of a compound direct object of the verb "watched" – I watched them and Spoade – but its placement at the end of the sentence has the effect of alienating him from the neatly controlled rhythms of the rest of the sentence. Spoade disrupts the order of his mind and of his syntax because he reminds Quentin of discomfiting conversations about homoeroticism and about virginity, a train of thought he passively follows back home to Jefferson to yet another version of his all-consuming conversation with his father. As he moves backward toward that conversation he loses control of syntax and cohesion:

> Calling Shreve my husband. Ah let him alone, Shreve said, if he's got better sense than to chase after the little dirty sluts, whose business. In the South you are ashamed of being a virgin. Boys. Men. They lie about it. Because it means less to women, Father said. He said it was men invented virginity not women. Father said it's like death: only a state in which the others are left and I said,

> But to believe it doesn't matter and he said, That's what's so sad about anything: not only virginity and I said, Why couldn't it have been me and not her who is unvirgin and he said, That's why that's sad too; nothing is even worth the changing of it, and Shreve said if he's got better sense than to chase after the little dirty sluts and I said Did you ever have a sister? Did you? Did you? (78)

Fragments of conversations at Jefferson and at Cambridge crowd confusingly together in a near complete breakdown of cohesion in the desperation of the paragraph's final sentences. The breakdown signals the loss of the carefully controlled observation of the world outside his window that began the passage. Reaching the juxtaposition of "little dirty sluts" and "sister," however, Quentin realizes he is on dangerous ground and quickly jerks himself back, away from this direction, and into a new paragraph, an ordered and detailed description of Spoade that forces him into the midst of the crowd, contains and controls him both poetically and syntactically by making Spoade over into a turtle, the very model of static nonaggression: "Spoade was in the middle of them like a terrapin in a street full of scuttering dead leaves" (78).

As with Hamlet, all things inform against Quentin, linguistically and visually. In spite of all he can do to keep Cambridge and environs on his tongue and in his mind, they nevertheless become a verbal and visual replication of Jefferson; nearly everything that takes place on June 2, 1910, brings him insistently back to scenes of pain at home. Many commentators have noted how the language and imagery of numerous scenes in Cambridge, especially the episode involving the little Italian girl, run parallel to Quentin's world at home. Even the veil-wearing women recruited by Gerald and Mrs. Bland for their picnic, named Miss Holmes and Miss Daingerfield, remind him – and readers – homophonically how fraught with danger and pain his home has been for him.

But even in the most lucid passages, Quentin's thoughts are constantly under siege, constantly on the verge of raveling out into disorder, so that a typical paragraph is likely to start a different thought, a new direction for him, like the new paragraph about Spoade, and then fall apart, as the chaos of things on his mind constantly presses for his attention, gets it, and leads him down dangerous paths of association. The section's second paragraph is a striking example:

> It [father's watch] was propped against the collar box and I lay listening to it. Hearing it, that is. I dont suppose anybody ever deliberately listens to a watch or a clock. You dont have to. You can be oblivious to the sound for a long while, then in a second of ticking it can create in the mind unbroken the long diminishing parade of time you didn't hear. Like Father said down the long and lonely light-rays you might see Jesus walking, like. And the good Saint Francis that said Little Sister Death, that never had a sister. (76)

This paragraph, and the following one, begin by focusing on something in the present moment and end, through loose but definite associations, at the same point in his past: the fact that he *had* a sister. As nearly every commentator has noted, Quentin's memory hovers, beggarlike, around his memories of what he thinks of as Caddy's abandonment of him in his need. The fifth paragraph is also particularly illustrative of the way his mind works:

> If it had been cloudy I could have looked at the window, thinking what he said about idle habits. Thinking it would be nice for them down at New London if the weather held up like this. Why shouldn't it? The month of brides, the voice that breathed *She ran right out of the mirror, out of the banked scent. Roses. Roses. Mr and Mrs Jason Richmond Compson announce the marriage of.* Roses. Not virgins like dogwood, milkweed. I said I have committed incest, Father I said. Roses. Cunning and serene. If you attend Harvard one year, but dont see the boat-race, there should be a refund. Let Jason have it. Give Jason a year at Harvard. (77)

This paragraph is almost a palindrome, which moves into and then out of the abyss of Caddy's wedding by the same route. Quentin begins by noting that he cannot look out the window because the sun is creating shadows that make him conscious of time. He thinks therefore of the boat races that his father has advised him to see, then realizes that the weather is pretty because it is June, which, he cannot help remembering, is traditionally the "month of brides." This realization, in turn, carries him back into another mélange of fragments, a breakdown of syntactical control, an italicized reversion to Caddy's wedding and its announcement, and a forced reentry back into roman type. He confronts his memory of Caddy's wedding with a memory of his verbal efforts to stop that wedding (his confession of their incest) – that is, with an effort to control Caddy linguistically, as he had been able to contain Spoade – and gradually builds back to where he started, his father's advice about the boat race, something in the present moment.

Italics here, and throughout Quentin's section, do not function as they do in Benjy's section; in most instances, they represent Quentin's farthest remove from language; as for Benjy they are visual images, rather than verbal ones, pictures welling up in his mind rather than articulated, or articulatable, descriptions of his feelings. Note, for example, how the italicized image of the street lamps in Jefferson blurble up so regularly throughout Quention's section, accreting up to the scene, fully recounted toward the end of the section, in which he and his father walk toward town, holding one of the conversations Quentin is so desperate to repress. In this paragraph the visual, even sensual, markers of Caddy's wedding intrude on his verbalization of things, and the italics represent a quick, perhaps instantaneous, scansion of what he saw and felt then, not what he is saying about it; those are things that he really doesn't want to put into words.

III. Jason

Jason abrupts on to the page and very nearly into the reader's ear with a very wet sense of humor so rich in the vernacular you can almost hear him speak. He may be, as Faulkner wrote sixteen years later in the Appendix, and as most commentators have taken too easily for granted, "the first sane Compson since Culloden" (342), but his monologue is very much of a piece with those of his brothers. For all the apparent "logic" of his outpourings, he too is driven by irrational forces buried deep in his unconscious that are battering at the boundaries of articulation. His monologue is a long loud agonizing cry – Benjy's howling rage made verbal – which he sustains at such a frenetic pace to drown out the voice of his unconscious, to silence its insistent pounding at the edges of consciousness with the earsplitting volume of the sound of his own voice. As Irena Kałuża has pointed out, it is

> devastatingly characteristic of Jason that he never allows his mental experience to operate beyond the conscious speech level, and always tries, by indefatigably inserting words like *because, when, where* and *if,* to organize his experience logically. But the result is far from logical, and his efforts are futile. Thus he always aspires to rationality without ever achieving it in fact.[11]

If Benjy is nonverbal and trying to say, and if Quentin is extremely verbal and trying *not* to say, trying to maintain order by keeping his words inside his head, Jason is intensely, loudly, desperately, gloriously oral. He keeps himself talking loudly so that he won't have to listen to the voices that threaten him: he drowns out one horrendous noise with an even more horrendous one.

One of the reasons Jason has been accepted as "saner" than his brothers is the relative normality of Faulkner's representation of his speech. His monologue almost completely lacks the visual markers, italics the most noticeable, of his brothers' incoherencies and psychic instabilities. It moves as much by associative logic as his brothers' monologues do, but because his psychic censor is much stronger than Quentin's, he is always able to stop himself just short of speaking that which he most fears, and thus manages to maintain a kind of control over his syntax – and so his psyche – that his brothers utterly fail at doing. But Jason cannot hide his diversionary tactics, and although Faulkner uses no italics in Jason's section, he still plays with the conventions of punctuation and representation in ways that reveal Jason's unconscious to us.

Jason's monologue can be characterized first by its defensive posture. His rhetoric is the most verbally aggressive in all of Faulkner. As Ross has noted,[12] he constantly uses his language to beat others into submission. He hardly ever engages in conversation, but rather in verbal combat, from which he can emerge a winner, because he is cleverer and quicker than most of his opponents (there are exceptions), who range from the members of his family to the functionary at the telegraph office. Although his rhetoric is aggressive, however, it emerges from a defensive mentality, perilously close to paranoia, that constantly screams self-justification. Jason is as obsessively aware of the constantly observing "eye" of his own conscience as his brothers are of the lighted window from their mother's room, and he engages a good deal of his psychic and verbal energy in defending himself from the accusations of idiocy and other forms of familial and genetic insufficiency that he imagines the people of Jefferson are constantly hurling at him (232–3, for example); his aggressive rhetoric is, in effect, a preemptory strike. And since he knows better than anybody else those points of character and blood where he is most vulnerable, he knows how to defend himself. We can thus discover his animating fears by paying close attention to the things he defends himself against.

A second rhetorical characteristic of Jason's monologue is its almost complete dependence on cliché.[13] Quentin's highly sensitive and poetic articulations of the world about him demonstrate considerable intellectual effort to keep his mind constantly, safely, and originally engaged with the externals of his final day in Cambridge. Quite to the contrary, Jason's language, though equally engaged with externals, is filled with clichés, aphorisms pious and secular, social and personal, mindless oral formulae that he can keep firing so rapidly because they come so easily to the tongue. They never require the speaker to question whether they *mean* anything; in fact they assume he will not. They are merely noise to fill the lacks in his gaps, as Addie Bundren might put it. Though they carry a good deal of the weight of a culture's traditions (its language anyway) and profess to embody a sort of folk wisdom, they nevertheless give only the illusion of meaning. Jason is so mired in these illusions that he is not even aware when they betray him, as in this passage: "After all, like I say money has no value; it's just the way you spend it. It dont belong to anybody, so why try to hoard it. It just belongs to the man that can get it and keep it" (194). Here flatly contradictory nostrums run amok, careen carelessly into each other and demonstrate both his hypocrisy and the mindlessness of his ravings. Jason clearly does not listen to what he says, and so his "sanity" cannot be demonstrated by his language. But for his purposes the words don't have to make sense so long as they make noise: what he cannot stand is the silence in which his real topic might articulate itself.

The quality of cliché is what gives his monologue its colloquial power, its roots in the spoken dialect, and its convincing orality, but the number of clichés also suggests the degree to which, for Jason, sound and sense are separated from each other. His mouth is estranged from his mind. He works very hard to force the disengagement, as we shall see, but in spite of all his efforts, he gets so caught up in the sound of his words that he has no idea what he is saying; he loses control of his words and, no less than Quentin, of his syntax. At such times, his guard down, his mind leads him directly back toward certain crucial moments in his psychic life. Like Quentin's monologue, Jason's hovers around these cruxes like moths around a flame, approaching disaster and then retreating, as the conscious and the unconscious do mortal battle with each other. Like Quentin's, Jason's guard occasionally does relax and, with his mind out of gear but his mouth constantly revving up one cliché after another, Jason rolls inevitably down the path of least resistance toward the precipitous edge, finally snatching himself safely away from it. At these moments of retreat from articulation Jason leaves huge narrative gaps that reveal his psychological preoccupations. As in the other brothers' monologues, Faulkner helps identify these preoccupations syntactically.

In certain ways he plays with the artifices of syntactical representation here more than he does in the first two monologues. Some of these ways can be demonstrated by noting a couple of differences between the 1929 Cape & Smith first edition text and the 1984 Random House New Corrected Text, which relies heavily on Faulkner's carbon typescript of the novel. Two passages are especially revelatory. The first occurs in a long funny diatribe that begins "Well, Jason likes work," and moves immediately to a by this point predictable litany into which Jason compresses all the objects of his anxieties by the same sort of fluid association characteristic of Quentin and Benjy. The association is very revealing. From this savagely ironic acceptance of his need to work, he jumps immediately to the reasons he has to work and like it, all revolving around the complex of circumstances he consciously sees as a betrayal of his chances to "get ahead" in life: Quentin's suicide, his father's death, Caddy's defalcation, Benjy's castration, and his mother's whining domination. He jokes about them to keep them at a distance:

> I says no I never had university advantages because at Harvard they teach you how to go for a swim at night without knowing how to swim and at Sewanee they dont even teach you what water is. I says you might send me to the state University; maybe I'll learn how to stop my clock with a nose spray and then you can send Ben to the Navy I says or to the cavalry anyway, they use geldings in the cavalry. Then when she sent Quentin home for me to feed too I says I guess that's right too, instead of me having to go way up north for a job they sent the job down here to me and then Mother begun to cry and I says it's not that I have any objection to having it here; if it's any satisfaction to you I'll quit work and nurse it myself and let you and Dilsey keep the flour barrel full, or Ben. Rent him out to a sideshow; there must be folks somewhere that would pay a dime to see him, then she cried more and kept saying my poor afflicted baby. (196)

Clearly Jason is in pain. Though he largely maintains control over his syntax, the energy of the passage suggests the pain is about to spill over into associations that he cannot control. He doesn't, for example, *name* Caddy, Quentin, or Father, although he does name his niece and Ben, who are the tangible, daily, reminders of his abandonment by the others. The passage continues, a few lines later:

> It's your grandchild, which is more than any other grandparents it's got can say for certain. Only I says it's only a question of time. If you believe she'll do what she says and not try to see it, you fool yourself because the first time that was the Mother kept on saying thank God you are not a Compson except in name, because you are all I have left now, you and Maury and I says well I could spare Uncle Maury myself and then they came and said they were ready to start. Mother stopped crying then. She pulled her veil down and we went down stairs. (196)

Jason's narrative here runs directly into, and then backs away from, a syntactical breakdown, as he realizes that he is approaching dangerously near one of his scenes of pain, his father's funeral. He still will not name Caddy, though clearly he is about to try to convince his mother that his sister will not keep her word not to see Miss Quentin. He starts to tell her how he knows Caddy won't keep her word by recalling her return to Jefferson for their father's funeral, but as he approaches the words "father's funeral," he realizes that he has entered dangerous territory:

> because the first time that was the Mother kept on saying

The Cape & Smith editors of the first edition, sensing that *something* was amiss, rendered this passage:

> because the first time that was that Mother kept on saying[14]

which neither corrects nor clarifies what is happening.[15]

Jason catches himself, just in time, from stumbling rhetorically into his father's grave. He starts to tell his mother that she can't trust Caddy because she lied "the first time" she promised never to try to see Miss Quentin again. Jason is on the verge of putting into words the scene of their confrontation over his father's grave, a scene triggered in his memory by the conversation with his mother about why he has to work, why he "likes" work. But he stalls. Faulkner's carbon typescript and his holograph manuscript render this passage as it appears in the 1984 New Corrected Text, and the passage is perfectly understandable as Faulkner wrote it if we try to hear Jason stumbling over his words. A more traditional novelist, using more traditional syntactical signs, might have rendered the passage as:

> because the first time – that was – the – Mother kept on saying.

This formulation would have visually approximated the rhythms of Jason's stumbling uncertainty at how to avoid what he is afraid he is about to say. Faulkner denies us the written punctuation that tells us how to *hear* Jason as he speaks, as he rushes blindly into a danger zone, halts, backs up, tries a couple of times to start over, and then finds a safer direction to pursue, he talking not *to* but rather *about* his mother.

He leaves Caddy's perfidy as a subject, but has in fact elided his narrative directly back to the funeral of his father – Jason, Sr., for whom he is named – in as fluid an associative movement as either of his brothers manages, except that his is more evasive. He finds a way to deal with his father's funeral on that rainy day, not by talking about Caddy but by focusing humorously, if savagely, on

Uncle Maury's drinking and on his feeble attempts to share in the burial in the rain. Father's funeral is the narrative locus for the next several pages, building toward that meeting with Caddy (196–207) at the cemetery, which he can now confront because he has constructed a self-justifying narrative framework that permits it. But his reconstruction has its own psychic rules. A telling moment occurs when he discovers that his uncle smells like clove stems, and that Maury is trying at least for the duration of the funeral to pretend that he is not drinking, though of course he is:

> I reckon he thought that the least he could do at Father's or maybe the sideboard thought it was still Father and tripped him up when he passed. (197)

This is the passage as it appears in manuscript, typescript, and the New Corrected Text; the first edition reads "at Father's funeral," which I believe indicates a misunderstanding of Faulkner's intent.[16] Jason simply will not put the words "Father's funeral" or "Father's grave" together, and again Faulkner refuses his readers the punctuation, the visual signs of reading – perhaps a dash following "Father's" – that would indicate how we are to *hear*, and so understand, what Jason is saying.

Throughout these pages, which also recount Jason's and Maury's participation in the actual digging of the grave, he refers to the grave only as "it." We cannot help but remember that Jason's first appearance in the novel is in the opening pages of the Benjy section, when Mrs. Compson, Benjy, and T.P. ride the buggy through town on the way to the cemetery. They stop at the store and ask Jason to accompany them, and he refuses. He is, after all, Jason *fils*, and the pain of his father's, and his own, mortality, looms large and threatening in his imagination. The rest of the passage (from the Jason monologue) is particularly illustrative of the way Jason's mind, and his language, work:

> After a while he kind of sneaked his hand to his mouth and dropped them out the window. Then I knew what I had been smelling. Clove stems. I reckon he thought that the least he could do at Father's or maybe the sideboard thought it was still Father and tripped him up when he passed. Like I say, if he had to sell something to send Quentin to Harvard we'd all been a dam sight better off if he'd sold that sideboard and bought himself a one-armed strait jacket with

> part of the money. I reckon the reason all the Compson gave out before it got to me like Mother says, is that he drank it up. At least I never heard of him offering to sell anything to send me to Harvard.
>
> So he kept on patting her hand and saying "Poor little sister", patting her hand with one of the black gloves that we got the bill for four days later because it was the twenty-sixth because it was the same day one month that Father went up there and got it and brought it home and wouldn't tell anything about where she was or anything and Mother crying and saying "And you didn't even see him? You didn't even try to get him to make any provision for it?" and Father says "No she shall not touch his money not one cent of it" and Mother says "He can be forced to by law. He can prove nothing, unless —— Jason Compson," she says. "Were you fool enough to tell –" (197–8)

Even though Jason forces a kind of logic on these associations, the passage really is a series of non sequiturs. The *becauses* are mechanical contrivances to connect them grammatically, but in fact the associations are emotional and nearly always lead him back to the same scenes of pain and conflict, whatever they happen to be. He and his mother refer to Caddy's daughter as "it," the same term he uses to refer to his father's grave, and doubtless they mean the same thing to Jason: his betrayal and abandonment by his father, his loss, like Quentin's, of an ordering center for his life. He would like to say "Father. Father."

There are similar passages in which his mother figures as the locus of a series of associated images. In the passage just cited, for example, Jason says "dam sight" rather than "damn sight," which as a visual, not an aural, distinction – eye dialect – is somewhat at odds with the intense orality of his narrative. One of the really curious orthographical features of Jason's rendered "speech" is that throughout this section Faulkner invariably employs "dam" rather than "damn" when Jason speaks on the page; that it was deliberate on Faulkner's part is suggested by the fact that when Jason quotes somebody else (Miss Quentin, twice on page 184, for example), he uses the normative "damn." The Cape & Smith first edition editors "corrected" "dam" to "damn" throughout Jason's section; when arguing for restoring Faulkner's carbon typescript reading in the New Corrected Text, I admitted that it was not clear why Faulkner did this, only that it was a demonstrable pattern, and I offered, rather feebly, the possibility that Faulkner was trying to make Jason's usage "less profane" than that of the others[17] but now that seems hardly likely. I would now suggest that Faulkner is creating a visual pun of the sort that confuses Benjy in the novel's second paragraph, and agree with Tom Bowden that the pun relies on a variety of maternal and animal-breeding meanings associated with the word "dam."[18] Faulkner uses "dam" to indicate how insistently "mother" and "sexuality" and even bestiality impinge on Jason's profanity and his attitudes, how profoundly they are related to his psychic problems; as a speaker Jason is no more aware of the difference in spelling than Benjy is of the difference between "Caddy" and "caddie," but the reader cannot escape it.

We can see how this works in another long paragraph, which occurs as Jason describes the beginnings of his futile search for his niece and the hated man in the red tie:

> I went on to the street, but they were out of sight. And there I was, without any hat, looking like I was crazy too. Like a man would naturally think, one of them is crazy and another one drowned himself and the other one was turned out into the street by her husband, what's the reason the rest of them are not crazy too. All the time I could see them watching me like a hawk, waiting for a chance to say Well I'm not surprised I expected it all the time the whole family's crazy. Selling land to send him to Harvard and paying taxes to support a state University all the time that I never saw except twice at a baseball game and not letting her daughter's name be spoken on the place until after a while Father wouldn't even come down town anymore but just sat there all day with the decanter I could see the bottom of his nightshirt and his bare legs and hear the decanter clinking until finally T. P. had to pour it for him and she says You have no respect for your Father's memory and I says I dont know why not it sure is preserved well enough to last only if I'm crazy too God knows what I'll do about it just to look at water makes me sick and I'd just as soon swallow gasoline as a glass of whiskey and Lorraine telling them he may not drink but if you dont believe he's a man I can tell you how to find out she says If I catch you fooling with any of these whores you know what I'll do she says I'll whip her grabbing at her I'll whip her as long as I can find her she says and I says if I dont drink that's my business but have you ever found me short I says I'll buy you enough beer to take a bath in if you want it because I've got every respect

> for a good honest whore because with Mother's health and the position I try to uphold to have her with no more respect for what I try to do for her than to make her name and my name and my Mother's name a byword in the town. (232–3)

This remarkable paragraph is as close to stream-of-consciousness as any in Quentin's monologue in its abandonment of all punctuation after Jason gets launched into the third sentence. As in other passages, Jason here compresses all his most threatening concerns: his father's drinking death, one brother's suicide, another's idiocy, his niece's sexual misconduct, his dalliance with his Memphis whore/girlfriend Lorraine, and his need to assert his own sexual potency, his physical mastery over women (his need to assure himself and others that he, unlike Benjy, does indeed have testicles), and, crucially, his paralyzing fear of the town's watchful eye. It is a mixture of important things, especially in the final lines where the syntax, on the verge throughout, breaks down completely: there is no object to the preposition "with," following the second "because," and no predicate to complete the clause that "because" begins. We notice this "because" since two of them, the only two in the paragraph, are jammed into this one sentence, whereas usually, as Kałuža has pointed out, Jason constantly uses such conjunctions to organize his speech, to force relationships, causes and effects, that may or may not exist; thus they signal a psychic association, if not a strictly logical or rational one. In this paragraph, "because" abrupts at us in that it becomes a psychic bridge between Lorraine and Mother: Mother equals whore.

Jason rumbles into this connection again later in a typically churning meditation:

> I'm a man, I can stand it, it's my own flesh and blood and I'd like to see the color of the man's eyes that would speak disrespectful of any woman that was my friend it's these dam good women that do it I'd like to see the good, church-going woman that's half as square as Lorraine, whore or no whore. Like I say if I was to get married you'd go up like a balloon and you know it and she says I want you to be happy to have a family of your own not to slave your life away for us. But I'll be gone soon and then you can take a wife but you'll never find a woman who is worthy of you and I says yes I could. You'd get right up out of your grave you know you would. I says no thank you I have all the women I can take

> care of now if I married a wife she'd probably turn out to be a hophead or something. That's all we lack in this family. (246–7)

The entire paragraph moves from his resentment of his niece's embarrassing public sexual misconduct and his irritation at having to support her, to her mother's perfidy, which, he thinks, is why he has to work for a living. The meditation runs from yet another assertion of his masculinity to a cliché-ridden and phony defense of his women friends to a cliché-ridden and phony attack on social morality, to a defense of his secret sexual liaison with Lorraine (secret from his mother, at any rate, and from the prying eyes of the town). His uncontested thoughts then stampede him into a defense of his bachelorhood, for which, he claims to have told his mother, he blames her: "If I was to get married you'd go up like a balloon." His reported exchanges with his mother throughout may be as imaginary as the ones Quentin claims with their father.[19] What is significant about Jason's "conversations," however, are the contorted connections he makes, willy-nilly, between his bachelorhood, Lorraine, and his mother: again and again Lorraine and Mother collide, in the deepest, least conscious, parts of Jason's mind.

Benjy's attempts to "say" get him castrated. Quentin also directly associates sexuality, sexual shame, with language when he fantasizes castrating himself, so he can treat sexuality as he would Chinese, as a language he doesn't know (116). Like Quentin, what Jason cannot "say," what he cannot confront in language, is how much he both fears and desires his own castration and death: "That's a hog for punishment for you," he says of Benjy:

> If what had happened to him for fooling with open gates had happened to me, I never would want to see another one. I often wondered what he'd be thinking about, down there at the gate, watching the girls going home from school, trying to want something he couldn't even remember he didn't and couldn't want any longer. And what he'd think when they'd be undressing him and he'd happen to take a look at himself and begin to cry like he'd do. But like I say they never did enough of that. I says I know what you need you need what they did to Ben then you'd behave. And if you dont know what that was I says, ask Dilsey to tell you. (253)

> And if they'd just sent him on to Jackson while he was under the ether, he'd never have known the difference. But that would have been too simple for a Compson to think of. Not half complex enough. Having to wait to do it at all until he broke out and tried to run a little girl down on the street with her own father looking at him. Well, like I say they never started soon enough with their cutting, and they quit too quick. I know at least two more that needed something like that, and one of them not over a mile away, either. But then I dont reckon even that would do any good. Like I say once a bitch always a bitch. (263)

These two startling passages – the latter close to the end of Jason's section and so part of his peroration – suggest the degree to which Jason's interlocutor throughout has been mostly himself, and he the object of his own scorn. The first passage suggests his attempt to imagine his way into the sexually safe castrated haven of Benjy's mind and, like Quentin, to imagine what it would be like not ever to have had sexual urges; he concludes that "you," his libidinous self, his id, his constant interlocutor, needs castrating. In the second passage he proposes "two more" that need cutting: "one of them ... not over a mile away" has to be his father, whom he still will not locate verbally in the cemetery; the other, closer, can only be himself.

Thus it is not for nothing that Faulkner very carefully plants the charged word "complex" deep in the heart of Jason's final paragraph: Mother and sexuality are as essentially the subtext of his monologue as of his brothers' – Mother and sexuality and all the related substitutions and evasions that spiral outward from oedipal guilt: shame, self-loathing, the need for expiatory punishment: castration and death. No less than Quentin, Jason longs for a strong father who will force on the world a moral center around which all the fragmentation of his psychic life can cohere. If he is, as Carvel Collins argued long ago,[20] Faulkner's version of Freud's punitive superego, he also manifests his brother Quentin's essential oedipal conflicts and expresses the identical fears, though in him they emerge as rage, mostly at himself. He is a cauldron, a veritable inferno, of oedipal conflicts, containing within himself a raging id that has to deal with a bedridden mother whom it both desires and revolts from in shame and whom it cannot evade by substituting an absent Caddy or even the ever-present and insatiable daughter of Caddy; that must also deal with a draconian superego that insists on controlling the world, and his own libido, by punishing it appropriately – by killing it or at least castrating it – and with a surprisingly fragile ego, which no less than brother Quentin's both fears and desires castration – and death as the ultimate castration – as an appropriate punishment for one who has sinned as he has. He is therefore not so much a "negative" image of Quentin[21] as a complete replication of his brothers, both of whom he contains within himself, along with the raging, punishing Father he so desperately longs for. This may be why he inspires in the reader the most complex response of any of the brothers.[22]

IV. Shegog

One of the most interesting aspects of Faulkner's treatment of language in *The Sound and the Fury* is his depiction of dialect. Representing speech in writing is tricky in English because of the range of acceptable phonemes that can be represented by a single vowel and several consonants. I don't mean just regional variations, but the difference between short and long vowels, for example. Consider idiolects and it's easy to understand the nightmare any writer faces in attempting to render the sounds that characters make when pronouncing words. Linguists have a very precise method of transcribing speech sounds, but fiction writers rely on less objective methods of representing speech. Because pronunciation is so varied, even within a single region, the notion of a "standard" is a pedantic one which implies a "correctness" against which variations become perforce at worst "erroneous" and at best "curious" or "charming" or even "sinister" or "pretentious," depending on the class and character of the person whose speech is being rendered.

Thus writers consciously or unconsciously depict a speaker's class and character in the degree to which they render speech as standard or variant.[23] This is true when the writer represents differences in vocabulary and pronunciation – Luster's "rinktum" for "rectum" (70), for example, or something like "ribber" for "river" – but it is most noticeable in the use of eye dialect, wherein the spelling changes not the pronunciation of a word but merely the way it looks on the page – "ov" instead of "of" or "bekaws" instead of "because." The difference, the nonstandard variance, is, like the Caddy/caddie of the novel's opening page, like Jason's "dam" instead of "damn," and like the "watter" or "watter-milyuns" that Quentin and Jason use when quoting a black character, available only to a reader, a literate person, not to the hearer or the speaker who, in being assigned a nonstandard written form, is depicted as nonliterate and thus different from the reader and the writer. Linguistic distinctions are those of class, of cultural and psychological otherness; dialect becomes a sure way to place a character regionally, culturally, and socially, and authors can invest characters with respect or condescension, with sameness or otherness, through the representation of speech. All authors must choose how much dialect to use, how much is enough to suggest the flavor of region and class, how much will distract from other, more important things in the fiction: George Washington Harris's *Sut Lovingood Yarns,*[24] for example, uses an eye dialect so heavy as to be virtually a different written language altogether.[25]

Faulkner tends to work at the other end of the scale from Harris; in *The Sound and the Fury* he uses almost no eye dialect at all. Nearly all the dialect spellings offer variant pronunciation, and Faulkner is usually much more interested in suggesting variant pronunciation, and Faulkner is usually much more interested in suggesting variant pronunciation than in rendering it precisely. Benjy's nonverbal narrative records more black speech than the monologues of his brothers, and, given that he has often been taken as a camera and a tape recorder, it seems natural to assume that he would *hear* and so record black pronunciation in the fullness of their dialect. This is not the case. Curiously, Faulkner represents black speech in Benjy's section almost completely in standard English. When dialect spellings do occur in the Benjy section, they are seldom more complicated than Versh's "Whooey. Git up that tree. Look here at this squirl, Benjy" (6) and his famous "ahun [iron] gate" (6). In effect, just as he let his reader be confused over Caddy/caddie, Faulkner for the most part refuses to tell us through dialect spellings what Benjy *hears* and adds only a tiny bit of the flavor of dialect, including eye dialect. Surely Benjy does not *hear* Dilsey say "Yes, sir" to his father, as Faulkner records it, but rather something more like "Yassuh" or the "Yes, suh" that black characters use in the other sections. When he does record dialect, he only very gently suggests variance – as when Dilsey talks about "the Lawd's own time" (26) – perhaps to keep the reader visually reminded of time and place, of social and cultural realities that Benjy cannot be aware of. In thus divesting Dilsey and other black characters of heavy dialect in Benjy's aural register, Faulkner invests them with sameness rather than otherness, and so reflects Benjy's sense of the Gibsons as central to his experience, the degree to which they define normality for him.

Not so Quentin and Jason, who are intensely aware of those social and cultural realities, and whose conscious rendering of black language does indeed reflect their assumptions about class and character. Quentin, trying to come to terms with black-white relations at home as he observes black-white behavior in Cambridge, reports the speech of the black man at the railroad crossing in Virginia with moderate dialect: "Yes, suh. . . . Thanky, young marster. Thanky" (87), and he notes that Deacon switches his language to suit his audience. When Quentin interrupts his conversation with a group of students, Deacon says to them, "See you again, fellows. . . . glad to have chatted with you." Turning to address Quentin, he gives the Southerner what he, Deacon, thinks the Southerner expects, and Quentin, in registering his speech, captures Deacon's exaggerated Southern dialect: "Yes, suh. Right dis way, young marster, hyer we is. . . . Hyer, boy, come hyer and git dese grips. . . . Now, den, dont you drap hit. Yes, suh, young marster, jes give de old nigger yo room number, and hit'll be done got cold dar when you arrives" (97). Quentin understands completely what Deacon is doing, and renders his dialect with some appreciation of Deacon's comic act, a timorous celebration of Deacon's otherness which all the while recognizes his impending and worrisome sameness. On the other hand, he treats Jefferson's Louis Hatcher, whose otherness is firmly fixed and nonthreatening, very paternalistically, and reports his speech with very condescending humor:

> Watter kin git des ez high en wet in Jefferson ez hit kin in Pennsylvaney, I reckon. Hit's de folks dat says de high watter cant git dis fur dat comes floatin out on de ridge-pole, too.... I cleant dat lantun and me and her sot de balance of de night on top o dat knoll back de graveyard. En ef I'd a knowed of aihy one higher, we'd a been on hit instead. (114)

Quentin does not hear Louis Hatcher say *watter* instead of *water*, any more than Benjy hears Dilsey say *Yes, sir*, but Faulkner writes it this way, one of the very few examples of eye dialect in the novel, to suggest Quentin's attitude toward Hatcher. Later, Faulkner turns Quentin's condescension around on him, invests *him* with otherness, when, after Quentin's conversation in absolutely standard English with the swimming boys outside of Cambridge, he hears one of them observe that he "talks like a colored man" (120)! Quentin does not comment on this irony, if he recognizes it.

Quentin's rendering of black pronunciation is mild compared to Jason's. Old Job, Jason reports, is going to the carnival in spite of Jason's ridicule:

> "I dont begridge um. I kin sho afford my two bits....
>
> "Dat's de troof," he says. "Well, ef I lives twell night hit's gwine to be two bits mo dey takin out of town, dat's sho." (231)

But even Jason is capable of distinctions, and so Dilsey, much closer to him than Job, gets a dialect a good deal less heavy than Job's: " 'And whar else do she belong?' Dilsey says. 'Who else gwine raise her cep me? Aint I raised ev'y one of y'all' " (198)?

Thus the nonverbal Benjy, so frequently assumed to be an objective tape recorder of sorts, makes no claim on verisimilar reproduction of the nonstandard sounds of his black keepers' speech. The two oral brothers do make such claims and, as we have seen, their rendering of dialect pronunciation changes according to their attitudes toward and relationships with the speakers being quoted. By far the heaviest dialect in *The Sound and the Fury*, however, occurs in the decidedly *written* and consciously *literary* fourth section, whose only pretense at orality is in the characters who are quoted and especially in the central oral narrative of section four, Reverend Shegog's Easter Sunday sermon. The writer-narrator of the fourth section uses a visual representation of Dilsey's language that strives for greater verisimilitude than even Jason's monologue does, and so moves toward a written language near that of George Washington Harris:

> "I'll have de fire gwine in a minute, en de water hot in two mo. . . ." "Luster overslep dis mawnin, up half de night at dat show. I gwine build de fire myself. Go on now, so you wont wake de others twell I ready." (268)

> "Whut you doin in de cellar?" she said. "Dont stand dar in de rain, fool," she said. . . .
>
> "Dont you dare come in dis do widout a armful of wood," she said. "Here I done had to tote yo wood en build yo fire bofe. Didn't I tole you not to leave dis place last night befo dat woodbox wus full to de top?" (269)

The verisimilitude threatens to reduce Dilsey and other black characters in the novel to the plastic black characters of Joel Chandler Harris, those of the popular imagination, in ways that Benjy's narrative does not. The further the point of view distances us from her, the stranger Dilsey appears to us. It's a striking illustration of just how "other" Dilsey is to Quentin and Jason – to the "narrator" of this section, and to us.

Thus as the novel moves toward more and more consciously and self-consciously "narrated," that is, written, materials – from Benjy's simple registering of sense impressions, through his brothers' much more complex sense of a psychic or social audience, to this narrator's more traditional audience of readers – the closer we come to a complete breakdown in the representation of words, and so in their capacity to convey meaning. The movement is completely parallel to the way Quentin's mechanical control over his language gradually breaks down as he loses psychic control of his life.

It is also completely parallel to the linguistic movement of Shegog's sermon which, at the center of the fourth section, is the novel's fourth oral narrative. It is Shegog's purpose to invest this life with meaning, to make it signify something instead of nothing in the midst of all the sound and fury. He locates this meaning in the life and death of Jesus Christ, and his sermon is a ritualistic incantation of that meaning for the assembled congregation, a meaning in which the congregation participates, though not in words: "Mmmmmmmmmmmmmmmmm!" they say, "Jesus! Little Jesus!" (296), and they do this "without words, like bubbles rising in water" (296). They are rapt; they lose themselves and become a collective not in or because of his words, but because of his voice: They seem to watch him, in a passage many commentators have noted, "with its own eyes while the voice consumed him, until he was nothing and they were nothing and there was not even a voice but instead their hearts were speaking to one another in chanting measures *beyond the need for words*" (294; my italics).

That *meaning* is not, for Shegog or the congregation, an articulatable one; it is *beyond words,* and he understands that no matter how much he tries to say, he and his communicants cannot communicate when they share signifiers alone, which shrivel away linguistically to nothing – their "Mmmmmmmmmm" is very close to Benjy's wordless moaning – but only when they share the signified itself. Since they share the ricklickshun and de blood, they need not refer to it at all. Like Deacon, Shegog reads his audience accurately, senses quickly that his very proper Northern diction will not do for this group of Southerners, and moves immediately from the standard "brethren," with which he first addresses his hearers in a "level and cold" voice (293) directly into heavy dialect:

> Breddren en sistuhn. . . . I got de ricklickshun en de blood of de Lamb! . . . Wus a rich man: whar he now, O breddren? Wus a po man: whar he now, O sistuhn? Oh I tells you, ef you aint got de milk en de dew of de old salvation when de long, cold years rolls away! (295)

His sermon is a hodgepodge of pseudo-eloquence and non sequitur and nonsense theology – he speaks of the "widowed God" (296), for example, and talks of "*seeing*" "de golden horns shoutin down de glory" (297) – which perhaps move by some sort of fluid stream-of-conscious associations in Shegog's mind, perhaps not. His rhetorical need, like Jason's, is to keep himself and his congregation wrapped up in his voice, which takes them "into itself" (295),[26] to keep the sound at such a pitch that there will be no time, no reason, for his congregation to think or articulate or explain. The closer he gets to meaning, the further he gets from standard language, from the signification of words, written or oral.

At the center of his sermon, at the center of his meaning, framed by all this oral non-sense, is the image of a motionless, silent *pietà:* the Logos, the very Word itself in the arms of a mother who cannot protect it from danger. Shegog's meaning cannot be evoked by the normal signifiers of their language, but by ritualistic communal incantations which evoke the visual icons of their belief. Like Benjy – it is not coincidental that he is sitting in their midst; in a linguistic sense, the novel here comes full circle – they bypass the obfuscation of signifiers and go, with Shegog, to a direct, unfiltered experience of that which is being signified. They can only do this when language breaks down completely, and they need not rely on it for the communication of their deepest beliefs: Jesus, in this frame, is in effect a signified which *cannot have* a sufficient signifier. They call him "Jesus," but no one believes that that mere sound carries the full significance of the image any more than the sounds "Caddy" or "caddie" or "*[kædI]*" contain for Benjy the full significance of his sister. In this context we can understand how words are, indeed, "sound and fury, signifying nothing." In this ecstatic moment, Benjy's fellow worshippers don't need *to say* because they share, because they believe: they absolve themselves of time and place, of social and cultural circumstance, of deep psychic wounds and urges, of guilt and recrimination, of all complexity. They can do this only for a brief respite, and only by focusing their hearts on the Word-less images of an idealized maternal love, of salvation and resurrection and hope that Shegog's sermon evokes. For the moment that is enough, and that is why the scene, with all its loud clashing and clanging, stands nevertheless so powerfully peaceful, almost serene, in contrast to the verbal armageddons of the Compson brothers' monologues, where articulation and meaning always meet as ruthless and inexhaustible antagonists.

NOTES

1 William Faulkner, *The Sound and the Fury.* New Corrected Text (New York: Modern Library, 1992). This text appends "Compson: Appendix: 1699–1946." Further citations contained in parentheses in the text refer to the edition.
2 John T. Matthews. *The Play of Faulkner's Language* (Ithaca: Cornell University Press, 1982), p. 75.
3 Stephen M. Ross, *Fiction's Inexhaustible Voice: Speech and Writing in Faulkner* (Athens: University of Georgia Press, 1989), p. 44.
4 Lockyer, Judith. *Ordered by Words: Language and Narration in the Novels of William Faulkner* (Carbondale: Southern Illinois University Press, 1991), p. 53.
5 Irena Kałuža, *The Functioning of Sentence Structure in the Stream-of-Consciousness Technique of William Faulkner's "The Sound and the Fury"* (Kraków: Nadładem Uniwersytetu Jagiellońskiego, 1967), pp. 49–50.
6 Lockyer, *Ordered by Words,* p. 53.
7 André Bleikasten, *The Most Splendid Failure: Faulkner's The Sound and the Fury* (Bloomington: Indiana University Press, 1976), p. 86.
8 Kałuža, *Functioning of Sentence Structure,* p. 52.
9 Noel Polk, *An Editorial Handbook for William Faulkner's The Sound and the Fury* (New York: Garland, 1985), pp. 8–12.
10 Ross, *Fiction's Inexhaustible Voice,* pp. 173–4.
11 Kałuža, *Functions of Sentence Structure,* p. 100.
12 Ross, *Fiction's Inexhaustible Voice,* p. 170.
13 Bleikasten, *Most Splendid Failure,* pp. 164–5.
14 Faulkner, *The Sound and the Fury* (New York: Jonathan Cape and Harrison Smith, 1929), p. 244.
15 Polk, *Editorial Handbook,* p. 63.
16 Ibid., p. 63.
17 Ibid., pp. 15–16.
18 Tom Bowden, "Functions of Leftness and 'Dam' in William Faulkner's *The Sound and the Fury." Notes on Mississippi Writers* 19 (1987): 81–3.
19 Matthews, *Play of Faulkner's Language,* p. 103; see also François Pitavy, "Through the Poet's Eye: A View of Quentin Compson." In André Bleikasten, *William Faulkner's The Sound and the Fury: A Critical Casebook* (New York: Garland, 1982), p. 93.
20 Carvel Collins, "The Interior Monologues of *The Sound and the Fury."* In Alan S. Downer, ed., *English Institute Essays 1952* (New York: Columbia University Press, 1954), pp. 29–56. Reprinted in James B.

Meriwether, ed., *The Merrill Studies in The Sound and the Fury* (Columbus, Ohio: Charles E. Merrill, 1970), pp. 59–79.

21 Bleikasten, *Most Splendid Failure*, p. 152.

22 Ibid., pp. 148–9.

23 Ross, *Fiction's Inexhaustible Voice*, pp. 104–5.

24 New York: Dick & Fitzgerald, 1867. Faulkner had a copy of this volume in his library at Rowan Oak.

25 Ross, *Fiction's Inexhaustible Voice*, p. 99.

26 See Ibid., pp. 40–5.

Notes on Contributors

Richard Godden, Senior Lecturer in American Studies at Keele University, is the author of *Fictions of Capital: The American Novel from James to Mailer* (1990) and of other essays on American and British literary topics.

Donald M. Kartiganer, The William Howry Professor of Faulkner Studies at the University of Mississippi, is the author of *The Fragile Thread: The Meaning of Form in Faulkner's Novels* (1979) and of numerous essays on Faulkner.

Noel Polk, Professor of English at the University of Southern Mississippi, is the author of *A Study of William Faulkner's "Requiem for a Nun"* (1981) and *An Editorial Handbook for William Faulkner's The Sound and the Fury* (1985).

Dawn Trouard, Director of Women's Studies and Professor of English at the University of Akron, has published essays on Faulkner, Eudora Welty, and other American literary figures. She has edited *The Eye of the Storyteller* (1989), a book of essays on Eudora Welty.

Selected Bibliography

The texts of *The Sound and the Fury* used throughout this volume are those of the "New, Corrected Edition," published by Random House in 1984 or a facsimile reprint of this edition published in differing formats by Vintage International (1987) and The Modern Library (1992), which appends the Compson Appendix that the 1984 and 1987 texts omitted. This new, corrected text was prepared by the present editor from Faulkner's typescripts and manuscripts, and readers may want to consult the facsimile reproductions of those documents in *William Faulkner Manuscripts 6: "The Sound and the Fury"* (2 vols.), ed. Noel Polk (New York: Garland, 1987), as well as Polk's *An Editorial Handbook for William Faulkner's The Sound and the Fury* (Garland, 1985), a detailed discussion of the texts and the considerations which went into each editorial decision.

Fully annotated listings of Faulkner criticism may be found in Thomas L. McHaney's *William Faulkner: A Reference Guide* (Boston: G. K. Hall, 1976) and John Bassett's *William Faulkner: An Annotated Checklist of Criticism* (New York: David Lewis, 1972) and Bassett's update, *Faulkner: An Annotated Checklist of Recent Criticism* (Kent, Ohio: Kent State University Press, 1983). Analytical surveys of the criticism are James B. Meriwether's "William Faulkner" in *Sixteen Modern American Authors: A Survey of Research and Criticism,* ed. Jackson R. Bryer (New York: Norton, 1973, pp. 223–75) and the update by Philip G. Cohen, David Krause, and Karl F. Zender in "William Faulkner," *Sixteen Modern American Authors. Volume 2: A Survey of Research and Criticism since 1972,* ed. Jackson R. Bryer (Durham: Duke University Press, 1990), pp. 210–300. The annual Spring issue of the *Mississippi Quarterly* now offers the most complete annual listing of work on Faulkner.

The items below have been selected for their usefulness in the study of *The Sound and the Fury.*

Aiken, Conrad. "William Faulkner: The Novel as Form." *Atlantic Monthly* 144 (November 1939):650–4. In Hoffman and Vickery.

Beck, Warren. "William Faulkner's Style." *American Prefaces* (Spring 1941):195–211. In Hoffman and Vickery.

Bleikasten, André. *The Most Splendid Failure: Faulkner's The Sound and the Fury.* Bloomington: Indiana University Press, 1976.

ed. *William Faulkner's The Sound and the Fury: A Critical Casebook.* New York: Garland, 1982.

Blotner, Joseph. *Faulkner: A Biography.* 2 vols. New York: Random House, 1974. Revised. 1 vol. New York: Random House, 1984.

Brooks, Cleanth. "Primitivism in *The Sound and the Fury.*" In Downer, pp. 5–28.

William Faulkner: The Yoknapatawpha Country. New Haven: Yale University Press, 1963.

Burnham, James. "Trying to Say." *Symposium* 2 (January 1931):51–9.

Coindreau, Maurice-Edgar, Preface to his translation of *The Sound and the Fury, Le bruit et la fureur.* Paris: Gallimard, 1938. In *The Time of William Faulkner,* ed. and chiefly translated by George M. Reeves. Columbia: University of South Carolina Press, 1971.

Collins, Carvel. "The Interior Monologues of *The Sound and the Fury.*" In Downer, pp. 29–56. Revised in James B. Meriwether, ed., *The Merrill Studies in The Sound and the Fury.* Columbus, Ohio: Charles E. Merrill, 1970, pp. 89–101.

"Biographical Background for Faulkner's *Helen.*" In *Helen: A Courtship and Mississippi Poems.* New Orleans and Oxford: Tulane University and the Yoknapatawpha Press, 1981, pp. 9–105.

Dickerson, Mary Jane, " 'The Magician's Wand': Faulkner's Compson Appendix," *Mississippi Quarterly* 28 (Summer 1975):317–37.

Downer, Alan S., ed. *English Institute Essays 1952.* New York: Columbia University Press, 1954.

Faulkner, William. "Appendix: Compson: 1699–1946." *The Sound and the Fury. New, Corrected Edition.* New York: Modern Library, 1992, 327–48.

Faulkner in the University, ed. Joseph Blotner and Frederick L. Gwynn. New York: Vintage, 1965.

Introduction to *The Sound and the Fury.* In Bleikasten, *Casebook,* pp. 7–14.

"The Kingdom of God." *New Orleans Sketches,* ed. Carvel Collins. New York: Random House, 1958, pp. 55–60.

Lion in the Garden: Interviews with William Faulkner 1926–1962. New York: Random House, 1968.

Mayday. South Bend, Ind.: University of Notre Dame Press, 1978.

Selected Letters of William Faulkner, ed. Joseph Blotner. New York: Random House, 1977.

The Sound and the Fury. New York: Cape & Smith, 1929; New York: Modern Library, 1946; New York: Vintage, 1956; New, Corrected Text, New York: Random House, 1984; Vintage, 1987; Vintage International, 1989; Norton, 1990; Modern Library, 1992.

Thinking of Home: William Faulkner's Letters to His Mother and Father, ed. James G. Watson. New York: Norton, 1992.

Gregory, Eileen. "Caddy Compson's World." In *The Merrill Studies in The Sound and the Fury*, ed. James B. Meriwether. Columbus, Ohio: Charles E. Merrill, 1970, pp. 89–101.

Gresset, Michel. "Psychological Aspects of Evil in *The Sound and the Fury*." *Mississippi Quarterly* 19 (Summer 1966):143–53.

Gwin, Minrose C. "Hearing Caddy's Voice." In *The Feminine and Faulkner: Reading (Beyond) Sexual Difference*. Knoxville: University of Tennessee Press, 1990, pp. 34–62.

Hicks, Granville. "The Past and Future of William Faulkner." *The Bookman* 74 (September 1931):17–24.

Hoffman, Frederick W., and Olga Vickery, eds. *William Faulkner: Three Decades of Criticism*. New York: Harcourt, Brace & World, 1963.

Irwin, John T. *Doubling and Incest/Repetition and Revenge: A Speculative Reading of Faulkner*. Baltimore: Johns Hopkins University Press, 1975.

Kartiganer, Donald M. "*The Sound and the Fury*." In *The Fragile Thread: The Meaning of Form in Faulkner's Novels*. Amherst: University of Massachusetts Press, 1979, pp. 3–22.

Kinney, Arthur, ed. *Critical Essays on William Faulkner: The Compson Family*. Boston: G. K. Hall, 1982.

Le Breton, Maurice. "Technique et psychologie chez William Faulkner." *Études Anglaises* 1 (September 1937), pp. 418–38.

Lester, Cheryl. "To Market, To Market: *The Portable Faulkner*." *Criticism* 29 (Summer 1987):371–92.

Lowrey, Perrin H. "Concepts of Time in *The Sound and the Fury*." In Downer, pp. 57–82.

Matthews, John T. "The Discovery of Loss in *The Sound and the Fury*." In *The Play of Faulkner's Language*. Ithaca: Cornell University Press, 1982, pp. 63–114.

The Sound and the Fury: Faulkner and the Lost Cause. Boston: Twayne, 1991.

Millgate, Michael. "*The Sound and the Fury*." In *The Achievement of William Faulkner*. New York: Random House, 1966. Reprint, Athens: University of Georgia Press, 1990, pp. 86–103.

O'Donnell, George Marion. "Faulkner's Mythology." *Kenyon Review* 1 (Summer 1939): 258–99. In Hoffman and Vickery.

Pitavy, François. "Through the Poet's Eye: A View of Quentin Compson." In Bleikasten, *Casebook*, pp. 79–99.

Ross, Stephen M. "The 'Loud World' of Quentin Compson." *Studies in the Novel* 7 (Summer 1975):245–57. Reprinted in Bleikasten, *Casebook*, pp. 101–14.

Sartre, Jean-Paul. "A propos de 'Le Bruit et la Fureur': la temporalité chez Faulkner." *Nouvelle revue française* 52 (June 1940):1057–61; 53 (July) 147–51. In Hoffman and Vickery.

Scott, Evelyn. *On William Faulkner's The Sound and the Fury.* New York: Jonathan Cape & Harrison Smith, 1929. In Kinney, pp. 115–18.

Sundquist, Eric J. "The Myth of *The Sound and the Fury.*" In *Faulkner: The House Divided.* Baltimore: Johns Hopkins University Press, 1983, pp. 3–27.

Thompson, Alan R. "The Cult of Cruelty." *Bookman* 74 (January–February 1932):477–87.

Thompson, Lawrance R. "Mirror Analogues in *The Sound and the Fury.*" In Downer, pp. 83–106.

Vickery, Olga W. "Worlds in Counterpoint: *The Sound and the Fury.*" In Vickery, *The Novels of William Faulkner: A Critical Interpretation.* Baton Rouge: Louisiana State University Press, 1959 (rev. 1964), pp. 28–49.

Printed in the United States
64331LVS00002B/98

9 780521 457347